WE WANTED WORKERS

ALSO BY GEORGE J. BORJAS

Friends or Strangers:
The Impact of Immigrants on the U.S. Economy

Heaven's Door:
Immigration Policy and the American Economy

Labor Economics

Immigration Economics

GEORGE J. BORJAS

WE WANTED WORKERS

UNRAVELING THE IMMIGRATION NARRATIVE

W. W. Norton & Company | NEW YORK | LONDON

Independent Publishers Since 1923

For information about special discounts for bulk purchases, please contact
W. W. Norton Special Sales at specialsales@wwnorton.com or 800-233-4830

Manufacturing by RRD Harrisonburg
Book design by Brooke Koven
Production manager: Julia Druskin

ISBN 978-0-393-24901-9

W. W. Norton & Company, Inc.
500 Fifth Avenue, New York, N.Y. 10110
www.wwnorton.com

W. W. Norton & Company Ltd.
Castle House, 75/76 Wells Street, London W1T 3QT

1 2 3 4 5 6 7 8 9 0

TO JANE

Contents

WE WANTED WORKERS

1

Introduction

THE PAST FEW decades have witnessed a historic integration of the United States into the world economy—even more so than in the first half of the twentieth century. This integration, an important element of the worldwide process of globalization, was marked by a rapid increase in the quantity of goods traded with other countries *and* in the number of people who immigrated to the United States. Between 1970 and 2015, the value of exports and imports as a fraction of gross domestic product (GDP) almost tripled from 11 percent to about 30 percent. The foreign-born share in our workforce tripled as well, from 5 percent to over 16 percent.

Not surprisingly, immigration and international trade have much in common. Both involve the movement of *something* across national boundaries. In the case of trade, manufactured goods are shipped from one country to another. In the case of immigration, persons themselves move across those boundaries.

It is easy to think of the international flow of goods as a kind of immigration. Consider what it means to import a proverbial widget. That widget did not create itself out of thin air. It was manufactured by a combination of physical resources and some labor. Making a single widget in China may require a high-skill worker to spend six months doing the design work and two low-skill workers to spend a full year molding a shapeless piece of metal into a desirable object. In a sense, importing a Chinese-made widget resembles the immigration of a high-skill Chinese worker for half a year, and the immigration of two low-skill Chinese workers for a full year. Put differently, immigration seems like trade, except that instead of importing the finished widget, we are importing the raw labor that can manufacture that widget domestically.

This equivalence between the international movement of workers and the international movement of goods influences the way in which many of us think about immigration. Countries might want to fill specific labor needs to produce things that the indigenous population desires, and immigrants provide the raw labor inputs that can be moved around from place to place to fill those needs. We often hear that the United States needs low-skill workers to harvest its lettuce and mow its lawns, and high-skill workers to write its software and teach at its universities. An almost infinite number of foreign-born low-skill workers is available to fill those low-skill job openings, and many high-skill workers seem willing to move to write code and teach.

Within this very myopic perspective, immigrants fill the labor slots that need filling, and those foreign-born workers play no other role in our country's cultural, political, social, or economic life. Our children's schools are unaffected, the welfare state is untouched, the balance of political power is unchanged, and daily life in our neighborhoods continues as before.

The accumulated knowledge from decades of research implies that international trade, on the whole, can have very beneficial impacts on the US economy, creating an instinctive bias toward viewing this type of "worker migration" favorably. We already know that international trade is beneficial for many. Therefore, the argument goes, admitting the much-needed foreign-born workers to fill the production slots must also be beneficial. After all, importing workers seems equivalent to importing widgets.

In the 1950s, this perspective led West Germany (and other European countries) to actively recruit and import hundreds of thousands of "guest workers" from Turkey and elsewhere. The guest workers were expected to be widget makers and nothing more. In other words, West Germany viewed those workers as the raw labor underlying the economic argument that immigration, like trade, must be beneficial. They were not considered to be part of Germany in any cultural or civic sense, and the German-born children of those widget makers were not even entitled to become German citizens until the 1990s. In the short term, the imported workers performed their assigned task: they produced widgets, and they produced them efficiently and by the millions. The contribution of those guest workers to the West German economy was likely an important factor in the postwar German economic miracle.

However, the presumed economic gains that result from looking at the world through the myopic lens of immigrants as a collection of robotic workers often clash with reality when we view immigration from a much broader and longer-term perspective. Over time, the impact of the "temporary" workers who would come in for a year or two to fill slots in the assembly line was not simply the sum of their contribution to widget production. By 2011, Turkish immigrants and their children comprised almost 4 percent of the German population, and the question of how the immigrants and their descendants fit into German society had become a central policy concern there. Reflecting on the European experience with the millions of guest workers, the Swiss playwright and novelist Max Frisch made perhaps the single most insightful observation about immigration when he quipped: "We wanted workers, but we got people instead."*

One underlying theme of this book is that viewing immigrants as purely a collection of labor inputs leads to a very misleading appraisal of what immigration is about, and gives an incomplete picture of the economic impact of immigration. Because immigrants are not just

---

* The exact quote is "Wir riefen Arbeitskräfte, es kamen Menschen." See Ulas Sunata, *Highly Skilled Labor Migration: The Case of ICT Specialists from Turkey in Germany* (Berlin: Lit, 2011), 275.

workers, but people as well, calculating the actual impact of immigration requires that we take into account that immigrants act in particular ways because some actions are more beneficial than others. Those choices, in turn, have repercussions and unintended consequences that can magnify or shrink the beneficial impact of immigration that comes from the contribution to widget production.

For instance, it is self-evident that not every person in a sending country wants to be an emigrant. People often choose to stay in their place of birth, despite the sizable economic gains to be had by moving from one place to another. The movers almost certainly differ in significant ways from the stayers; they have different motivations, different capabilities, and so on. To calculate the impact of immigration correctly, it is not just a matter of counting the number of bodies that filled the slots in the proverbial widget factory. We also need to worry about *which* types of persons the receiving country ended up attracting. It would not be surprising if a receiving country, channeling Max Frisch's observation through Obi-Wan Kenobi, concluded that perhaps "those were not the workers we were looking for."

Once the immigrants settle in their destination, they have many more choices to make. If immigration were simply the process of placing workers along the assembly line, we would not need to worry about the assimilation prospects of the immigrant population. The workers fill the factory slots, and it does not matter much whether they learn the language and embrace the cultural, social, and political norms of their new homes.

However, immigrants are people, and people make choices. A crucial choice that all immigrants must make is whether to assimilate into their new surroundings. As Europe is learning, assimilation does not happen automatically, and a large unassimilated population presents many challenges. From an immigrant's point of view, assimilation has many benefits; for example, an immigrant may find better-paying jobs. But there are also many costs; for example, an immigrant has to devote time to learning the new language, or may have to give up long-held cultural traits and beliefs. Immigrants are more likely to

assimilate when conditions on the ground make it in their best interest to do so.

The immigrant-as-worker perspective also does not seem to allow
immigrants to procreate, but people surely do. The descendants of
the immigrants and the descendants of those descendants guarantee
that the impact of current immigration will continue into the far-
off future. Moreover, real-world immigrants wear an ethnic label.
They cluster in ethnic enclaves that influence their integration and
that have many social and political consequences. Because different
groups of immigrants might pursue different assimilation paths, the
second and third generations may be raised in ways that lead them to
fully embrace the culture and norms of the receiving country, or they
may not.

Perhaps the melting pot will fully incorporate the descendants
of today's immigrants into the native population, as it did with the
descendants of the Ellis Island arrivals in the early 1900s. But it could
also be that the long-term integration of those earlier immigrants was
the result of cultural, political, and economic conditions specific to
the United States during the twentieth century, and it may be difficult
to duplicate those conditions in other places and at other times.

Immigrants also have an economic impact through their contributions to or use of the welfare state. The myopic immigrant-as-worker
perspective ignores the fact that immigrants have lives outside the factory gate. But immigrants get sick, have accidents, lose homes, win
lotteries, and are subjected to the same random twists of fate that we
all face. And, just like us, many will need help and assistance when
bad things happen.

The welfare state in the United States is designed to provide assistance not only to those who are most needy, but also to the working
poor. And it is obvious that a broader perspective of immigration—one
that views immigrants as something more than robotic workers—implies
that the impact of immigration on the public treasury will depend on
who the immigrants are. If the people who choose to migrate are
high-skill workers, immigration will benefit the fiscal bottom line;

the immigrants will add little to the cost of maintaining the welfare state and will share the burden of funding it, including helping to pay for the substantial costs resulting from an aging native population. But if the immigrants are low-skill workers, immigration could increase the fiscal burden for natives.

In short, there are crucial differences between an evaluation of immigration that relies on the immigrant-as-worker metaphor and one that takes the broader perspective that immigrants are people. But there are important similarities as well. In either case, immigrants increase the size of the workforce, and this "supply shock" changes conditions in the labor market. Most obviously, an increase in the number of people who can do a particular type of work will likely reduce the wage that employers need to offer to people looking for that work. At the same time, however, other people will gain; after all, lower wages for the workers typically mean higher profits for the employers. In the end, immigration will almost certainly improve the economic well-being of some Americans, but other Americans will be worse off.

The broader perspective that views immigrants as people, rather than as an army of worker robots, has a key implication: the fact that immigration had this particular impact at this particular time in this particular place does not guarantee that the same will happen the next time we see a supply shock. Put differently, there does not exist a magic formula for mechanically predicting what will happen the next time a sizable group of people decides to move from one country to another. Much will depend on the factors that generated the new flow and on the conditions that the immigrants encounter in their new home.

We Wanted Workers summarizes what we learn about the *economic* impact of immigration on the United States once we view it from this broader perspective. Although I am myself an immigrant, this is not an ideological sermon on immigration; there is no attempt to moralize or to either canonize or demonize immigrants. Instead, a recurring refrain is that the economic consequences of immigration are not evenly distributed among the many people that immigration affects. Put simply, some people win and some people lose. Devoid of all the ideological trappings and all the deliberate obfuscations, immigration can be viewed for what it plainly is: another redistributive social policy.

Under some conditions, the grand total of the gains accruing to the natives who win will exceed the grand total of the losses suffered by the natives who lose, so that immigration (like international trade) increases national wealth. It is also entirely possible that these gains could be greatly reduced or even reversed by other real-world circumstances, such as the fiscal burden that may arise from excessive immigrant participation in public assistance programs or the social costs resulting from an unassimilated foreign-born population.

Instead of leading to grand universal statements, the broader and more realistic approach forces us to think about what determines the economic impact of immigration and to isolate the various factors that can make immigration either more beneficial or more costly. That approach also helps to identify the groups that win and the groups that lose. In the end, these insights could be used to formulate an immigration policy that, if the United States wanted to, would make immigration more advantageous and would more evenly spread the gains and losses.

I HAVE BEEN working in the trenches of immigration research in economics for about three decades. As part of this work, I have constructed intricate mathematical models and theories of immigration and examined data sets containing millions of people to try to document the economic impact.

This book is my attempt to summarize in a very accessible way how we know what we think we know about immigration, to provide an easy-to-follow account of how we reach those conclusions, and to highlight the caveats that are often hidden in dense footnotes and raise questions about whether the conclusions and assertions deserve our trust. An awareness of how these "facts" came about provides a much better understanding of what we truly know and a much better sense for how we should proceed.

When I first began working on this topic in the early 1980s, immigration was not a central concern either in economics or in discussions of US social policy. In fact, it would be fair to characterize immigration research in economics as being in the backwater of professional interest. And it is also fair to characterize the debate over immigration policy as nothing more than a detectable (but growing) concern over illegal immigration.

Times have certainly changed. Immigration has now become perhaps *the* most divisive political issue of our time. And immigration research has become a central focus of interest among labor economists (those of us who specialize in examining how labor markets work). Hundreds of published academic studies examine various aspects of the immigration puzzle.

These two threads of interest feed off each other. As the political debate heated up, there was increasing demand for information that could be used to frame the discussion and, particularly, to support specific policy positions. Obviously, where there is demand—and especially where there are funds for researchers to conduct such studies—there will be supply, and a rapidly growing number of economists now work on immigration-related issues. The number of research studies is now so large that it would take a few months of careful reading to become familiar with the various themes. It probably would take even longer to fully appreciate the subtleties built into the theories and statistical methods that are commonly used to frame and answer the questions.

Paul Collier, a renowned British public intellectual and a professor at Oxford University, published a book in 2013 entitled *Exodus: How Migration Is Changing Our World*. Collier himself had never conducted research on immigration issues in his academic work; instead, he had written a number of influential books on such diverse topics as the impact of government aid to poor countries and the politics of global warming. The main point of *Exodus* is that the presumed large benefits that immigration can impart to receiving countries may be greatly reduced as the number of immigrants increases substantially and the migration flow continues indefinitely. Large and persistent flows, Collier argued, could have many other (sometimes harmful) unintended consequences.

Regardless of how one feels about this conclusion, I found it particularly insightful to read Collier's overall perception of the many social science studies that he reviewed as he prepared to write the book:

> A rabid collection of xenophobes and racists who are hostile to immigrants lose no opportunity to argue that migration is bad for indigenous populations. Understandably, this has triggered a reaction: desperate not to give succor to these groups, *social scientists have strained every muscle to show that migration is good for everyone.*[1]

This is as damning a statement about the value of social science research on immigration as one can find. As far as I know, Collier is the first distinguished academic to state publicly that social scientists have attempted to construct an intricate narrative that shows the measured impact of immigration to be "good for everyone."

I have never made such an assertion in public. But I have long suspected that a lot of the research (particularly, but not exclusively, outside economics) was ideologically motivated, and was being censored or filtered to spin the evidence in a way that would exaggerate the benefits from immigration and downplay the costs.

Many conceptual assumptions and statistical manipulations can affect the nature of the evidence. A computer program that analyzes data from a survey of millions of persons can have hundreds, if not thousands, of lines of code, and a seemingly innocuous programming assumption here or sample selection there can lead to very different results. Moreover, dissecting a published study to isolate precisely which conceptual assumption or statistical manipulation may be responsible for a specific claim involves a lot of time and effort, and there is little professional reward for playing detective.

We Wanted Workers argues that it is crucial to carefully examine the nuts and bolts of the underlying research before one can trust the claims made about the impact of immigration. I will try to make the discussion of the data that are often used in immigration research, and how those data are manipulated, as transparent as it can possibly be. The book, in fact, will provide various examples in which arbitrary conceptual assumptions, questionable data manipulations, and a tendency to overlook inconvenient facts help build the not-so-subtle narrative that Collier detected.

In addition, given the standing charge that social scientists who study immigration may have an ideological predilection that guides the research, and given that the angle I pursue in this book definitely deviates from the narrative—stressing instead that although immigration may be good for some, it is not necessarily good for all—perhaps it is important to provide a bit of background on my own life history. My personal story will allow the reader to ascertain where exactly I am coming from, and why my views have evolved in ways that depart from the politically correct narrative.

I was born in Cuba and migrated to the United States with my mother just two days after turning twelve in 1962. I cannot recall ever hearing anyone in my family discuss the possibility of migrating to the United States prior to Fidel Castro's takeover in 1959. Perhaps it was because my father was seriously ill throughout my childhood, putting the notion of moving anywhere else far outside our set of potential actions. But there did not seem to be all that much interest in even visiting the United States. No one in my extended family had ever visited the country before the revolution.

My family owned a small garment factory that manufactured men's pants, and that provided a comfortable, though far from wealthy, lifestyle. The factory had perhaps twenty or thirty workers, and many of those were family members. I am one of those rare economists who can say that I have spent much time inside a working factory where labor and capital manufactured a product that was sold in the marketplace—although much of my time in the factory was spent climbing very tall piles of neatly stacked pants ready to be shipped out.

Soon after the communist takeover, the factory was confiscated, and I recall the government trucks coming one day to pick up the sewing machines and equipment and leaving behind an empty, hangar-like space. The topic of immigration began to surface in family discussions, and it took on additional urgency after the rumor began to circulate that Castro was going to ship out all the children for a reeducation campaign in the countryside. My parents were determined to rescue me from that fate regardless of what it involved, and they were ready to ship me out of the country entirely on my own. My father's health, however, was deteriorating rapidly, and the timing never worked out.

The spring of 1961 marked two major events: my father's passing away and, very shortly after that, the debacle of the Bay of Pigs. I remember the morning of the failed invasion. We lived near a military base outside Havana, and planes zoomed down to attack the base. It was very early in the morning, probably 4:00 or 5:00 a.m., but the whole episode felt like a Hollywood movie, with the whizzing of the planes and the loud explosions. Later that day, or perhaps it was in subsequent days after life had returned to normal, the school bus that took me to one of the two prominent Catholic schools in Havana was stopped outside the gate.* Soldiers boarded the bus, and we were told that the school was permanently closed.

I was transferred to one of the local "revolutionary schools," where classes consisted almost entirely of listening to Marxist-Leninist nonsense taught by, it seemed to me, wild-eyed young men. I think my neurological system has never fully recovered from the shock of going from my introductory algebra class to learning about Marx, Lenin, and the Cuban Revolution. Nevertheless, I did well in the new cur-

---

* I was enrolled at the Colegio de La Salle; Fidel Castro was an alum of the other school, the Colegio de Belén.

riculum. I used to have an uncanny ability to memorize, regurgitate, and then completely flush from my brain all the gibberish that didn't belong there. In fact, my academic performance was impressive enough that I was quickly asked to join the marching band that participated in many official events, including cosmonaut Yuri Gagarin's visit to Havana. (I have often wished I could show my children a picture of my young self in full revolutionary regalia playing drums in front of the Cuban politburo.)

My time at the revolutionary school taught me two valuable life lessons. First, I intensely dislike ideological arguments. I have kept my distance from ideologues throughout my life—ranging from the hyperpartisan left-wing radicals that I so often encounter in academia to the rigid libertarians that seem to sprout and flourish in some quarters. Second, those wild-eyed teachers taught me to distrust authority and to be skeptical—*very skeptical*—of expert opinion. That cynicism of what experts manufacture and sell has stayed with me to this day.

After the events of spring 1961, it was only a matter of waiting for the exit permissions to be granted by the Castro regime, reserving spots on one of the twice-daily Havana-to-Miami flights operated by Pan American Airways, and having the entry visas approved by the United States. My mother and I finally emigrated on October 17, 1962. After some final harassment at the Havana airport, we boarded the morning flight and landed in Miami a short time afterward. Coincidentally, the day before, President Kennedy had been informed that the Soviets had placed medium-range ballistic missiles in Cuba. Within a week, the Cuban Missile Crisis engulfed the entire world in a frightening standoff, and the Pan Am flights that had carried so many Cubans to a brand-new life were permanently canceled, abruptly halting the exodus of refugees. This not-so-minor detail would spark my professional interest in immigration many years later.

Another lesson from those days came from my first experience at the administrative center that handled the paperwork for the newly arrived Cubans. Freedom Tower, near downtown Miami, acted as the Ellis Island for the refugees. As I recall, my mother and I visited the center a day or two after our arrival to get our papers in order and to fulfill whatever registration requirements we needed to fulfill. The officials were actively trying to get the Cubans to resettle outside the Miami area and were offering the new arrivals plane tickets and resettlement funds to get them to disperse more randomly across the country.

The officer who looked at our case decided that we should resettle in Los Angeles. To a twelve-year-old who loved movies, the notion of moving to California was extremely appealing, and I know that my mother was near the point of giving in and agreeing to the deal. At some point during the conversation, however, someone behind us yelled out a warning: *No vayan a California. Tienen terremotos.* ("Don't go to California. They have earthquakes there.") And *that* was the end of the resettlement conversation. I often remember this event, as I have spent a big chunk of my adult life building mathematical theories of immigrant behavior. Although the equations are helpful and let us see the big picture, I have always known in the back of my mind that what actually happens is not really determined by those equations. What actually happens often depends on somebody yelling out a random phrase like that one about the San Andreas Fault.

In Miami, we lived in a neighborhood that was about a third Cuban. Practically all my friends and acquaintances were Cuban, although I also had a couple of American friends at school. None of the refugees in that neighborhood had been wealthy enough to have the foresight or means to transfer out resources from Cuba prior to their exit. All of us had left with a few clothing items and little else. Despite the very disadvantaged status, I have extremely fond memories of early-1960s Miami. I soon had a bicycle, a sense of freedom that I have never been able to recapture, and my friends and I must have visited—totally unsupervised, of course—all the far reaches of Dade County.

Many of our neighbors were Cuban professionals who had little income but a lot of human capital and drive. Whenever I got sick, a neighbor who had been a physician in Cuba but now worked in a manufacturing factory would examine me, make a diagnosis, and "prescribe" some medicine. A sympathetic Cuban employee at the pharmacy would gladly—and without questions—fill the "prescription." I am certain that many of those doctors eventually reestablished themselves in the medical community in the United States and opened up very successful practices in the decades ahead.

In a similar vein, my mother quickly found work at a garment factory opened by a family acquaintance—an entrepreneur who had owned a competing pants factory in Havana, and who somehow had the wherewithal to start a very small operation in Miami. The work was low-paying and sporadic, but it gave my mother the opportunity to start building a new life in a country that she felt was her permanent home (unlike many of the other refugees, who believed that the Castro regime was surely just a temporary nightmare that would soon end).

Since those days, I have had a very affectionate perspective on immigrant communities, always mindful of how they provide an extremely generous and effective mechanism for helping a group of uprooted people navigate through very difficult times.

The poor employment opportunities that Cubans faced in Miami at that time soon led my mother to move to Hoboken, New Jersey, where two of her sisters had settled after getting out of Cuba. Hoboken then was not the gentrified New York City suburb that it is now. Instead, it was a poor town that had been a gateway for Italian immigrants in the early twentieth century (in fact, for a time we lived in a tenement across the street from the house where Frank Sinatra was born), and the recipient of a large flow of recent Puerto Rican migrants. But despite the change in ethnic background, I again witnessed the process of how immigrant communities manage, survive, and thrive.

Fast-forward a decade. It is the mid-1970s, and I am a graduate student at Columbia University studying for a doctorate in economics. My doctoral dissertation examines how the frequency and timing of changing jobs affects wages. Sometime in that period, economist Barry Chiswick presented an early draft of his work on the assimilation of immigrants at the Columbia Labor Workshop.[2] That workshop, founded by Gary Becker and Jacob Mincer, has a legendary history, simply because Becker and Mincer were the two economists most responsible for building the field of modern labor economics. Chiswick's presentation was certainly the first time I had seen or heard about an immigration-related research paper in economics. In retrospect, the Chiswick study gave birth to the modern study of the economics of immigration. The argument was simple and powerful: immigrants who have been in the United States for many years earn much more than recent arrivals do, indicating that there is a lot of economic assimilation.

I was obviously predisposed to find the topic interesting. During the presentation, I asked a question that summarized everything I knew about immigration at the time. Although hundreds of thousands of Cubans had moved to the United States, I knew that the flow was composed of two distinct waves. There were the Cuban immigrants, like myself, who had arrived mostly in those Pan Am flights before the missile crisis. And there were the Cubans who came years later, after other escape routes had been established. I was vaguely aware of rumors in the Cuban community that the two waves were different, with the earlier wave composed primarily of entrepreneurs and professionals, and the later wave containing many low-skill persons.[3] So my question was simple: How does the analysis take account of such situations? After all, the high earnings of the earlier immigrants may have little to do with assimilation, and instead may reflect that they are different kinds of people. I have no recollection of the ensuing discussion, but the question interested me and remained embedded in my brain for years.

Not until the early 1980s, after I had finally moved to California— earthquakes or not—did my professional interest in immigration issues surface. At the time, immigration was beginning to change California in fundamental ways, and the change was happening rapidly. My thoughts, for some reason, kept returning to the question that I had asked at that Columbia seminar years earlier. How exactly would one measure the assimilation of immigrants in a world where the different waves had different capabilities?

The motivation for my initial work in immigration, in fact, is typical of the way in which most of the key research papers that I have written on immigration got started. None of those studies had a policy concern as the seed. Typically, the issue that first attracted me was purely methodological: How exactly would one go about trying to find out this or that? Because I instinctively dislike ideological arguments, I also never felt the need to put much thought into how my work fit with the narrative that was slowly developing. My papers would describe how one would measure this or that, how one would think about this or that, and the answer would be whatever it was. Needless to say, that answer could be useful in policy discussions, but it was the solving of the puzzle, rather than the policy concern itself, that attracted me.

It did not take long for me to be reminded that my work was deviating from the narrative. My first paper on immigration was published in 1985, and its contribution (which will be discussed later in the book) was to answer precisely the question that I had asked at that Columbia seminar: What does the fact that earlier immigrants earn more than recent immigrants really imply?

Instead of interpreting the earnings gap as proof of assimilation, I proposed that perhaps it indicated simply that the waves that had arrived in the past were more skilled than the newer waves (as I had imagined was the case with the Cuban migration). I then derived a statistical methodology that would enable anyone to distinguish between the two alternative stories. The evidence reported in my study suggested that there had indeed been a long-term decline in the skills of immigrants, and that although there was some economic assimilation, it certainly was not as pervasive as the original Chiswick study had claimed.

A grant from the Rockefeller Foundation funded that initial research. I recall meeting one of the foundation's program managers at a conference, and I pointed out that it would be really interesting if

I could return to the historical data and reexamine the assimilation of the immigrants from the early 1900s. After all, a similar argument—that the new immigrants were not quite as "good" as the old—had been made at the time and heatedly debated. The reaction was a terse "Why would you want to open up that can of worms?" That experience was my first encounter with an attitude that I have now witnessed more times than I care to remember: some questions are better left unasked.

Fast-forward a few more years, and my work began to develop some notoriety; it was seen by some as being skeptical of immigration. My first book, *Friends or Strangers*, was published in 1990.[4] In it, I attempted to summarize what my research on immigration had uncovered up to that point. It was published at about the same time that Julian Simon published a far more technical book, *The Economic Consequences of Immigration.*[5]

Julian Simon was a renowned economist. He had made (and won) a famous bet about the future trend in the price of commodities with Paul Ehrlich, an equally renowned academic who has written extensively about the dangers of overpopulation.[*] Simon also was interested in immigration, becoming the "dean" of the pro-immigration libertarian lobby in economics. Soon after *Friends or Strangers* was published, Professor Simon warned me that my work was being interpreted improperly by those who were using some of the inconvenient facts summarized in the book in ways that did not further the narrative. He wrote me a letter, dated April 9, 1990:

> At a couple of meetings recently, anti-immigration people . . . as well as Congressman Lamar Smith of Texas, have quoted your book as supposedly showing that immigrants are bad for our econ-

---

[*] Simon and Ehrlich bet on whether the price of a group of commodities—chromium, copper, nickel, tin, and tungsten—would rise between 1980 and 1990. Ehrlich believed that overpopulation would create a shortage of natural resources and the price of commodities would surely rise. The price fell, and Simon won the bet.

omy. . . . I certainly find no warrant for the statements they make in your book. If you wish to be interpreted otherwise, you might write something to [name and address redacted], who goes to lots of meetings about immigration. After he reads a disclaimer from you once or twice, it might embarrass those who would use you to that effect.[*]

I am certainly glad that Professor Simon, after looking at *Friends or Strangers*, concluded that he could not find anything that would "warrant" the anti-immigration statements made on my behalf. At the time the book was written, for example, there was no credible evidence suggesting that immigration had harmful effects on native earnings—and I said so in no uncertain terms: "The methodological arsenal of modern econometrics cannot detect a single shred of evidence that immigrants have a sizable adverse impact on the earnings and employment opportunities of natives in the United States."[6] But the book pointed out that there had been a decline in the skill level of immigrants, and that the economic gains from immigration would be much larger if immigrants were more skilled.

I never did send the disclaimer that Professor Simon had suggested. Instead, I answered his letter a few days later by saying simply: "I don't really want to get into a long series of discussions as to what my book really means. I obviously can't respond to every single allegation by every single person who quotes it or cites it."

Julian Simon's out-of-the-blue request made a deep impression at the time. There was certainly a lot of pressure to make sure that the "correct" interpretation was attached to whatever academics were writing on immigration, lest the "xenophobes and racists" get the wrong idea and actually begin to cite data from research studies.

Despite those early bumps in the road, I continued to work on immigration issues (on and off, but mostly on) throughout my career.

---

[*] I have redacted the names of private institutions and persons who are not government officials.

I found the study of immigration much too fascinating to walk away from it entirely. Because the field of immigration economics had not yet matured, many questions were waiting to be addressed for the first time. And I truly was curious to find the answers to many of those questions, and ambitious enough that I wanted to be the first to get there. Fortunately, the early hurdles—and many others along the way—did not deter me from asking those questions and from seeking answers.

2

Lennon's Utopia

IN JOHN LENNON'S iconic *Imagine*, he urged his listeners to imagine a world without countries. He immediately followed this plea with the assertion that such a mental exercise would not be hard to do. I have been a lifelong Beatles fan, and I have a still-sealed copy of the "butcher" album acquired decades ago to prove it. But it is clear that Lennon's claim about how easy it would be to imagine life in his borderless utopia was far off base. What exactly would a world without national borders look like?

Economists have spent a lot of time trying to figure out what would happen if we got rid of the barriers that limit trade across countries. Much of the research on international trade is precisely an attempt to imagine the effects on employment, prices, and incomes if countries allowed unrestricted movement of goods and capital across national boundaries.

One common theme in this research, a theme that has greatly influenced economic policy, is that free trade increases global income and equalizes prices and wages across countries. Although free trade also creates winners and losers—just ask the American consumers buying cheap electronic goods or the American manufacturing workers competing with Chinese imports—it is widely accepted that the winners gain more than the losers lose. In other words, free trade makes countries wealthier *and* reduces global economic inequality at the same time.

Decades of experience with many trade liberalization policies, however, have not increased incomes or equalized wages as much as economists promised. At the time that the North American Free Trade Agreement (NAFTA) was being debated in the early 1990s, there were claims that the creation of a free trade zone in North America would substantially increase Mexican income and remove pressures for Mexican emigration. Those promises did not pan out. By 2004, a decade after the free trade zone was established, Nobel Prize–winning economist Joseph Stiglitz was writing:

> While the hope was that NAFTA would reduce income disparities between the United States and its southern neighbor, in fact they have grown—by 10.6 percent in the last decade. Meanwhile, there has been disappointing progress in reducing poverty in Mexico, where real wages have been falling at the rate of 0.2 percent a year.[1]

Similarly, the *New York Times* reported in 2007 that:

> The North American Free Trade Agreement held out an alluring promise: the agreement would reduce illegal immigration from Mexico. Mexicans, the argument went, would enjoy the prosperity and employment that the trade agreement would undoubtedly generate—and not feel the need to cross the border into the United States. But today the number of illegal migrants has only continued to rise.[2]

The failure of free trade to deliver on the promise of a much wealthier and more egalitarian world has inspired yet another generation of experts to imagine yet another scenario and make yet another set of promises: the removal of immigration restrictions that prevent the movement of people from one country to another will increase world income by tens of trillions of dollars and solve the world's poverty problem once and for all.

However, thinking about what would result from unrestricted international migration makes John Lennon's *Imagine* exercise much more difficult. What exactly would happen in such a world? How many people would move? What would economic conditions in the new borderless world look like? What would happen to the institutions and social norms that govern economic exchanges in specific countries after the entry or exit of perhaps hundreds of millions of people? Would the economic, political, and social institutions that helped produce the vast wealth in the richer countries remain dominant and spread throughout the globe? Or would these institutions be overwhelmed by the inefficiencies that hampered growth in the poorer countries?

Many of the additional difficulties arise from the simple fact that the movement of goods across national boundaries differs fundamentally from the movement of people. The movers are not simply raw labor inputs whose only role is to take a predetermined spot along the widget assembly line in their new homes. Instead, the movers are people who will inevitably have many unintended consequences, and who cannot be discarded after we extract their economic value the way we would throw away an old imported car or a broken imported widget.

The influential work of Canadian economists Bob Hamilton and John Whalley, published in 1984, was the first to consider a borderless world within the typical framework of viewing immigrants as robotic workers.[3] Their analysis, as well as much of the subsequent research, addressed a basic question: What would happen to global wealth if sovereign countries surrendered their ability to restrict immigration flows?

Needless to say, no real-world data exist that might help us estimate the impact of open borders. After all, many, if not most, mass migrations through the centuries were sparked by cataclysmic factors, including wars, social turmoil, political upheaval, and economic or environmental catastrophes. The histories of those migration flows, even if we could get accurate details on their impact, probably have little to say about what would happen if we eliminated all immigration restrictions today.

The lack of data, however, need not be that big a deterrent to an economist. We instead *imagine*. We turn to a mathematical model of a hypothetical world economy, a world that noneconomists might dismiss as "Fantasyland," and then plug in numbers to see what the repercussions of removing national boundaries would be. It turns out that the answer given by the standard way we think about how labor markets work is quite shocking: the global gains from the removal of immigration restrictions would be enormous, amounting to tens of *trillions* of dollars annually.

This discovery encouraged a new generation of advocates to assert that the "opening of borders is the world's greatest economic opportunity."[4] The promise is frequently wrapped in a vivid metaphor: there are trillion-dollar bills lying on the sidewalk, ready for the taking, if only the receiving countries would remove the self-imposed migration barriers.[5]

The creative manufacturing of those trillion-dollar bills highlights a number of issues and themes that recur frequently in the immigration debate. It is obvious, for example, that much will depend on whether we view immigrants as workers or immigrants as people. It is also obvious that we need to make assumptions to play this very difficult game of *Imagine*—and, needless to say, assumptions matter. Finally, any such game will produce many new insights. Some of those insights, however, detract from the narrative, and those are often hidden away in the attic of inconvenient truths.

1. WHERE DO THE GLOBAL GAINS COME FROM?

THERE IS ENORMOUS inequality in economic resources across countries. Some countries have large territories, vast natural resources, and few people, while other countries lack the land and natural resources, and its citizens live in overcrowded conditions. Some countries have an industrialized infrastructure that makes workers more productive, while the infrastructure in other countries lags decades behind. The populations of some countries share a set of values, behavioral norms, and political institutions that enhance productivity, while the populations of other countries lack those values, norms, and institutions. In view of all these differences, it is not all that shocking that per capita income differs dramatically, from about $40,000 to $50,000 annually in the United States and other industrialized countries, to about $8,000 in Paraguay and the Philippines, to less than $2,000 in Haiti, Ethiopia, and Malawi.

If international migration were not allowed, labor markets in the high-wage countries would face little pressure from immigrants looking for better job opportunities, and the income differences could persist for a very long time. Let's now take up John Lennon's challenge and imagine what would happen in a world without countries. Specifically, what would happen if all national boundaries were suddenly removed and people could move to any place they wanted?

It is easier to play this game if we simplify the rules a bit. For example, let's think of a world that has only two countries: the North, an industrialized and wealthy region, and the South, a developing and poor region. Suppose also that it costs nothing to move from one place to another, so no financial obstacles impede migration. And finally, all workers are equal in this world; they are all productive clones of each other. Everyone is a widget maker, living in a wonderful widget-producing and widget-consuming world.

The removal of immigration restrictions in such a world unleashes forces that will eventually equate the wage across countries. As long as the main incentive driving migration is the desire to improve one's economic well-being and the North pays a higher wage, people will want to move from the low-wage to the high-wage region. This movement will create upward pressure on the wage in the South, as employers must try a little harder to fill jobs with fewer workers, and will create downward pressure on the wage in the North, as employers have many more workers to pick from. In the end, employers in both the North and the South will pay exactly the same wage, and it will make no difference where a person works.

It turns out, however, that the unrestricted movement of workers across countries does much more than equate the wage in the two regions. A fundamental insight in economics, dating back to eighteenth-century Scottish economist Adam Smith's invisible hand, is that this voluntary movement also leads to the richest world possible.

To see why, let's imagine a slightly different scenario. Suppose that a dictator rules this world. The dictator's goal in life is simple: to make the world as wealthy as it can possibly be. And he has the power to allocate workers to whichever region he thinks best.

The dictator picks a worker from the South at random. Should he let the worker stay in the South or move the worker to the North? Because the dictator wants to increase global wealth, he places that worker where the worker will be most productive, the North. In fact, the dictator will keep dispatching workers to the North as long as productivity in the North exceeds productivity in the South. But this forced migration reduces the productivity of workers in the North (as the North gets ever more crowded) and raises the productivity of workers in the South (as labor in the South becomes more and more scarce). The dictator stops reallocating persons when the productivity of a worker is the same in the two regions, meaning that this dictator has rearranged the world's population so that it again makes no difference where a person works.

At the end of the dictator's day, the outcome is exactly the same as if people had moved voluntarily: conditions in the North and the South are identical. Put differently, the removal of immigration restrictions accomplished the dictator's goal: to make the world as wealthy as possible. And this is the economist's answer to John Lennon: a world with no countries would be a very wealthy world indeed.

This utopian outcome has a magnetic appeal to many libertarians, who often view the ideology of open borders as a fundamental tenet. The editorial board of the *Wall Street Journal*, for example, has called for the adoption of a five-word constitutional amendment that reads simply: "There shall be open borders."[6]

Actual calculation of the global gains from opening up the borders is very mechanical. Economists assume that the standard way we think about labor markets describes how the Northern and Southern labor markets interact in this hypothetical world. They then write down some equations to capture those insights, and finally they plug in numbers.

World Bank data enable us to construct the two regions in our game of *Imagine*. The high-income countries of the real world, with a population of 1.1 billion people and 600 million workers, make up the North. The real-world developing countries, with a population of 5.9 billion people and 2.7 billion workers, make up the South.

A key number that needs to be plugged into the exercise is how the wage reacts to supply shocks in both regions of this hypothetical world. The movement of, say, 100 million workers from the South to the North will increase the Southern wage by some amount and reduce the Northern wage by some other amount—but, by how much? A common assumption, discussed later in the book, is that a 10 percent drop in the number of workers in the South increases the Southern wage by 3 percent, and a 10 percent increase in the number of workers in the North reduces the Northern wage by 3 percent.

The other key number that needs to be plugged in is the one that summarizes the initial wage gap between the North and the South. This number is the mother lode of incentives for Southern workers to pack up and move. The productivity of a worker now employed in a developing country would increase, and perhaps increase dramatically, if he or she were suddenly placed in an industrialized economy. In fact, the wage of low-skill workers from many low-income countries would easily quadruple if they could move to the United States.[7]

In 2013, prior to the hypothetical opening of the borders, world GDP was about $70 trillion. As Table 2.1 shows, the removal of immigration restrictions would indeed lead to a huge increase in GDP: global wealth would increase by $40 trillion—almost a 60 percent rise.

TABLE 2.1. THE IMPACT OF OPEN BORDERS, 2013

Increase in world GDP	+$40.1 trillion
Number of migrant workers	2.6 billion
Number of movers, including family dependents	5.6 billion
Wage change in the North	−39.3%
Wage change in the South	+143.0%
Change in the income of capitalists	+57.2%
Increase in world GDP, accounting for moving costs	+$28.1 trillion

Source: George J. Borjas, "Globalization and Immigration: A Review Essay," *Journal of Economic Literature* 53 (2015), 965.

Moreover, the gain would accrue *each year* after the restrictions were removed, so that the total value of the accumulated gains would near a *quadrillion* dollars!

Given these astronomical numbers, it is not surprising that advocates are willing to engage in radical social engineering by promising that world poverty could be eliminated—if only countries would stop being countries. In other words, there are trillion-dollar bills lying on the sidewalk, ready to be picked up. All it takes is for policy makers in the industrialized countries to wise up and remove all immigration barriers.

Although the existence of those trillion-dollar bills is the main point emphasized by the open-border advocates, this particular game of *Imagine* has many other implications—and those additional implications do not see the light of day quite as often. For example, the *same* algebra that led to the predicted $40 trillion gain also implies that there will be an awful lot of movers. In fact, 2.6 billion workers, or 95 percent of the workforce in the developing countries, need to move to the North in order to equalize wages across the two regions. If these workers bring along their families, 5.6 billion persons will move from the South to the North.

The fact that practically the entire developing world needs to move is not all that shocking; the ability of a Southern worker to quadruple his wage by moving is sending a very powerful signal about productivity differences across countries. Some parts of the world are so inefficient at producing economic value that the exodus of persons searching for better opportunities would eventually empty those regions out.

It is fair to say that this particular implication of the model—that *billions* of people would need to move—has not received the same emphasis as the prediction that world GDP would increase by tens of trillions of dollars. For example, the original Hamilton-Whalley article spends a lot of time giving detailed estimates of the dollar gains, but curiously neglects to report the number of movers required to achieve those gains at *any* point.

Glossing over this number is the politically sensible thing to do if one wishes to advocate these types of models in policy circles. After all, *imagine* the reaction at a congressional hearing if an open-border advocate was asked how many immigrants the industrialized countries would attract and the reply was: "Oh, something over 5 billion people."

Some advocates might argue that a sizable gain could still be achieved even if only a fraction of the potential movers were allowed to move. For instance, global GDP would increase by $7 trillion if only 10 percent of the potential movers moved. This "modest" scenario would still involve the migration of 560 million persons. According to the United Nations, there are now 232 million immigrants in the entire world—the United States being the largest recipient, with over 40 million.* Achieving an increase in world GDP of $7 trillion requires a tripling of the existing number of immigrants worldwide.

---

* The five countries with the next-largest foreign-born populations are Russia, Germany, Saudi Arabia, the United Arab Emirates, and the United Kingdom, each with about 8–11 million immigrants.

Inevitably, in the open-border scenario, the huge migration flows will also produce a substantial redistribution of wealth, and the distributional consequences tend to be overlooked as well. After all, the wage equalization predicted by open borders means that *wages are equalized*: workers who initially have high wages end up earning less, and workers who initially have low wages end up earning more. In fact, the earnings of the North's native workforce will drop by almost 40 percent, while Southern workers will more than double their earnings. One last redistributive impact is worth mentioning— and again it is one of those nuisance statistics that is swept under the rug: the income of capitalists worldwide will increase by almost 60 percent.

In short, a world integrated by open borders creates very large gains for some groups (Southern workers and capitalists) and very large losses for a group of workers who will vociferously fight the policy shift. And their refusal to go along with the open-border advocates may have little to do with racism or xenophobia. Northern workers simply do not benefit from the New World Order.

Up to this point, the game of *Imagine* in this hypothetical world has assumed that people can move from the South to the North instantaneously and at zero cost—something akin to the way people are teleported in and out of the starship *Enterprise*. But we know migration is not costless, even under Captain Kirk's watch.

As we will soon see, all of the available evidence suggests that moving costs are very large. In fact, the cost of moving from one industry to another or from one country to another is perhaps eight to ten times a worker's initial salary. If a worker's moving costs are ten times his salary, and if the dependents can tag along for free, the last row of Table 2.1 shows that global gains drop from $40 trillion to $28 trillion simply because the gains must now net out the cost of moving billions of people. Nevertheless, even after accounting for sizable moving costs, the increase in world GDP is still in the tens of trillions of dollars.

2. PRODUCTIVITY SPILLOVERS

THINGS THAT SOUND too good to be true are usually false. And the 30–40 trillion-dollar bills lying on the sidewalk are some of those things. Those bills are as fake as Monopoly money.

The main problem with the promise that global wealth will increase by tens of trillions of dollars is that it comes from a very myopic game of *Imagine.* The game does not take into account how the industrialized economies will respond to the entry of perhaps billions of persons. We know nothing about how industrialized societies actually would react to such huge supply shocks. But it would be a mistake to interpret our ignorance as a sign that there will be no such reaction. After all, it is not billions of robotic workers that are moving around, but billions of *people.*

It is hard to believe that production in the industrialized world could continue along its current path. The entire social, political, and cultural balance in these societies will be rearranged after the population more than quintuples. Although some might argue that a slow pace of absorption would help minimize the disruption, the sheer number of movers makes it impossible to achieve the economic gains in a realistic time frame. For example, if the entire developed world were to allow immigration at *triple* the current rate in the United States, *it would still take 500 years for all the movers to move.*[*]

Most discussions of the benefits from high-skill immigration to the United States rely on the notion of "productivity spillovers"—the idea that high-skill immigrants can somehow permanently increase the productivity of native workers by exposing natives to new types of knowledge. Put differently, the neurons of native workers get stimulated when they hang out with exceptional immigrants. It is easy to

---

[*] The United States admits 1 million legal immigrants a year with a population of 320 million—an immigration rate of about 0.3 percent. If all developed countries, with a population of 1.1 billion, had an immigration rate of 1 percent, they would accept 11 million immigrants per year, and it would take 509 years to admit all 5.6 billion movers.

imagine that the notion of productivity spillovers reappears when we consider a supply shock involving the movement of billions of people. Unfortunately, the spillovers resulting from this massive migration flow would not be the same as those generated by high-skill immigrants.

In their influential and well-received book *Why Nations Fail,* Daron Acemoglu and James Robinson addressed the central question of why global inequality in the distribution of economic resources is so large and so persistent.[8] They argued that some nations succeed and some fail partly because of differences in political and economic institutions. Similarly, in *Exodus,* Paul Collier noted that "one reason poor countries are poor is that they are short of effective organizations" and "migrants are essentially escaping from countries with dysfunctional social models."[9]

For unrestricted immigration to produce those trillion-dollar bills, billions of people must be able to move to the industrialized economies without importing the institutions, the dysfunctional social models, the political preferences, and the culture and norms that led to poor economic conditions in the sending countries in the first place. It seems inconceivable, however, that the North's institutional, social, and political fabric would remain intact after the entry of billions of new persons. Collier bluntly summarizes the dilemma: "Uncomfortable as it may be . . . migrants bring their culture with them."[10]

One way to think about the potential impact of the spillovers is to imagine that immigrants do carry some baggage with them, and that baggage, when unloaded in the new environment, dilutes some of the North's productive edge. The baggage may include cultural attitudes toward work, a distinct political ideology, and social norms that favor or prohibit certain interactions.

We have no clue about how powerful the productivity spillovers would be. Nevertheless, we can keep playing the game John Lennon suggested and imagine what would happen if the productive advantage of the North were cut by, say, half. This is, in fact, what Table 2.2 does. It shows what happens to the predicted global gains after the North loses some fraction of its advantage.

TABLE 2.2. GAINS AFTER ACCOUNTING FOR
PRODUCTIVITY SPILLOVERS, 2013

	No spillovers	North loses 50% of its edge	North loses 75% of its edge
Change in world GDP (in trillions)	+$28.1	–$0.9	–$12.4
Change in North's wealth (in trillions)	+$11.9	–$4.5	–$13.0

Source: George J. Borjas, "Immigration and Globalization: A Review Essay," *Journal of Economic Literature* 53 (2015), 969. The simulations take moving costs into account.

If the spillovers reduced the North's productive edge by half, the promised $28 trillion dollar windfall (after accounting for migration costs) would turn into a trillion-dollar loss. If the productive edge were cut by 75 percent, global GDP would shrink by $12 trillion. This huge loss occurs because the spillovers ensure that practically the entire world's workforce will now operate under the set of inefficient organizations and institutions that were previously isolated in the South.

It is important to emphasize that *this is only a game of Imagine*— and one should put as much faith in these numbers as one puts on the promise that trillion-dollar bills lie strewn all over the sidewalk. The game, however, makes a point that is far too often ignored: the gains from open borders depend entirely on how the infrastructure in the industrialized world reacts to the influx of perhaps billions of persons.

The game also tells us why receiving countries staunchly ignore the advice of the experts. Each country probably enacts an immigration policy that is best for that country's national interest. Sometimes the decisions lead to policies that encourage the entry of high-skill workers, or favor relatives of earlier immigrants, or restrict the rights granted immigrants after arrival, including the right to vote or the right to move internally within the country.

But *why* are the receiving countries acting so foolishly? *Why* do policy makers in those countries refuse to enact policies that presumably would increase their wealth?

The answer is both trivial and profound: the receiving countries know something that eludes the experts. The receiving countries know that removing all immigration restrictions may provide few gains, and there is a chance of a very large loss. For instance, we can calculate how much income actually accrues to the North (to both workers and capitalists) after the immigrants' salaries are paid. As Table 2.2 shows, the gain to the North would be $12 trillion if there were no productivity spillovers. But those 12 trillion-dollar bills quickly turn into a $5 trillion loss if the immigrants take away just half of the North's productive edge. In short, the productivity spillovers can easily turn a rich country's expected windfall from open borders into an economic debacle.

It is useful to drive home this point by imagining open borders in a very specific setting: the modern Middle East. Israel's economic prowess stands out in that conflict-ridden region. The World Bank reports that per capita GDP in Israel was $32,000 in 2013, compared to $11,000 in Egypt, $12,000 in Jordan, about $15,000 in both Iraq and Iran, and $17,000 in Lebanon.

What would happen to aggregate wealth in the Middle East if all migration restrictions were removed within that subset of countries? There are obvious economic incentives for people to move to high-wage Israel. In fact, an economic model without productivity spillovers would predict sizable gains for the aggregate Middle East—perhaps in the tens of billions of dollars—as persons moved from low-wage countries to high-wage Israel.

However, *there will be spillovers*. The spillovers arise from the key distinction between the migration of robotic workers and the migration of people, the actual human beings who work, consume, pray, procreate, vote, fight, and so on. It is easy to imagine that a Middle

East with open borders would make the promise of billion-dollar bills on the sidewalk a tragic joke.

Even though I have hung around economists my entire adult life, I am still surprised by the zeal with which some cling to their models. I have posed this Middle East example to some in the open-border camp and just asked: What do you *really* think would happen if there were open borders? The reply is typically a regurgitation of the insights suggested by the model of the hypothetical world economy (Middle Eastern GDP would increase) and totally ignores the realities on the ground.

Economic models are useful, but they have limits. I suspect that receiving countries know exactly what they are doing when they disregard the promises of the open-border advocates and instead build walls.

3. IMMIGRATION AND SOCIAL CAPITAL

AS I MENTIONED earlier, the discussion in *We Wanted Workers* focuses on the *direct* economic effects of immigration. The fact that immigrants affect the receiving country in many other ways— changing social customs, the norms that guide everyday interactions, the cultural milieu, and the political environment—will remain hidden in the background, even though these consequences themselves have an economic impact. As we have seen, the productivity spillovers in John Lennon's utopia raise the possibility that the cost of these societal changes might overwhelm whatever direct economic benefits immigrants generate.

There is little doubt that immigrants bring their own culture and that the importation of those norms has consequences. One well-known study examined the parking habits of diplomats in New York City and showed, in a very simple context, how cultural spillovers can have social and economic repercussions.[11]

Until 2002, a diplomat's illegally parked car could be ticketed for a traffic violation, but a diplomat who did not bother to pay the ticket could not be punished in any way. Even though all diplomats in New

York City, if they wished to abuse the system, had free parking anywhere and at any time—making a diplomatic plate "the best free parking pass in town"—only some of them *chose* to ignore the rules that apply to everyone else. This situation raises an interesting question: *Which* foreign diplomats assigned to the United Nations ignored traffic rules and committed parking violations, such as parking in a no-parking zone?

Between 1997 and 2002, the five countries with a sizable diplomatic staff (at least ten diplomats) and the largest number of violations per diplomat were Egypt, Senegal, Pakistan, Ivory Coast, and Morocco. All of these countries had between 60 and 140 violations per diplomat during the period. The countries with *zero* violations included Australia, Colombia, Japan, Norway, and Turkey.

The variation in parking violations across diplomats from different countries showed an interesting pattern: the diplomats who originated in countries that were characterized by high levels of corruption were much more likely to park illegally, be ticketed, and ignore the fine. The obvious interpretation is that diplomats bring some of the baggage that characterizes social interactions back home, and that baggage influenced their behavior in New York City, affecting a small part of the social fabric that holds the city together.

And, of course, natives react to the importation of whatever is being imported. Robert Putnam, the prominent Harvard political scientist, has reported some controversial and discouraging evidence about the native response.

In his celebrated book *Bowling Alone*, Putnam argued that Americans were increasingly isolated, and that this isolation resulted in a fraying of the social network and ties that bind the community together—which could be thought of as a decline in "social capital."[12] The decline in trust and cooperation documented in *Bowling Alone* made Americans worse off, impairing our ability to achieve personal and social goals.

In subsequent work, Putnam examined how the growing ethnic and racial diversity in our country was affecting social capital. In a widely cited study, Putnam reported the results of a survey carried out in a large number of communities, ranging from Los Angeles to Boston to South Dakota to West Virginia. The evidence was surprising and striking. In Putnam's words:

> Immigration and ethnic diversity tend to reduce social solidarity and social capital. New evidence from the US suggests that in ethnically diverse neighbourhoods residents of all races tend to "hunker down." Trust (even of one's own race) is lower, altruism and community cooperation rarer, friends fewer.[13]

Putnam goes on to provide a long list of the seemingly harmful effects of increased ethnic diversity: lower confidence in government, lower voter registration rates, a lower probability of giving to charity or volunteering, and a lower chance of participating in community projects. Although Putnam speculates that some of these adverse effects may fade in the long term, as immigrants build communities and form new identities, the actual data is unequivocal: ethnic diversity reinforces the fraying of the social networks that played such a central role in *Bowling Alone*. Putnam is fully aware of the implications for the narrative that immigration is good for everyone: "It would be unfortunate if a politically correct progressivism were to deny the reality of the challenge to social solidarity posed by diversity."[14]

It would be deceptive to argue that ethnic diversity can lead to only harmful consequences. Increased diversity almost certainly broadens our horizons, making us see and understand the world in different ways, and that new outlook can be very beneficial in social and economic interactions. Ethnic diversity also broadens the range of products available to US consumers, generating additional gains along the way. However, we simply do not know what the aggregate impact of immigration would be if we tallied all potential social consequences and compared them to the direct economic effects that are the focus of this book. Our ignorance arises partly because the existing studies have examined but a small subset of all possible social effects. But, more important, we do not have a way of converting the social and cultural impact into a consistent dollars-and-cents measure.

One thing, however, is certain. Advocating policy shifts that lead to massive migration flows or that rearrange the world order—such as the adoption of open borders—without being able to fully predict or even to understand the eventual impact of that rearrangement seems premature and irresponsible. It could even turn out to be a misguided attempt at do-gooding with devastating consequences. If nothing else, the deconstruction of the promise that open borders will generate enormous economic gains teaches a lesson worth remembering: beware of experts whistling the enchanting harmonies of John Lennon's *Imagine* while tossing fake trillion-dollar bills onto a mythical sidewalk.

3

How We Got Here

WE NOW ZOOM in from the panoramic perspective offered by the open-border scenario to the US context. Economist Richard Easterlin evokes the significance of immigration to the United States with a simple statement: "The magnitude of immigration to America is unmatched in the history of mankind."[1] Since the settlement of Jamestown in 1607, over 92 million foreigners have migrated to the territory that makes up our country.*

The statutes that regulate legal immigration to the United States are thought to be nearly as convoluted (and almost as long) as the Internal Revenue Code. The complexity feeds an industry of immigration lawyers whose job is to provide visa applicants "safe passage" through the many bottlenecks in the system. Judges in the federal courts frequently acknowledge the complexity of immigration law:

---

* The Department of Homeland Security reports that 79.5 million persons were legally admitted between 1820 and 2013, and that 11.4 million undocumented immigrants live in the country. About 800,000 persons migrated to America prior to 1820; see Raymond L. Cohn, "Immigration to the United States," *Economic History Association Encyclopedia*, 2015. The counts do not include the African slaves who were involuntarily transported to the United States.

We are in the never-never land of the Immigration and Nationality Act, where plain words do not always mean what they say.[2]

This case vividly illustrates the labyrinthine character of modern immigration law—a maze of hyper-technical statutes and regulations that engender waste, delay and confusion for the government and petitioners alike.[3]

Because of this complexity, it would take volumes to precisely summarize the intricate web of statutes and regulations that decide who can receive a visa and who cannot. Nevertheless, a bird's-eye view of the evolution of immigration policy is useful, as it showcases the landmarks that have determined the winners and losers of the immigration lottery throughout the nation's history.

1. LEGAL IMMIGRATION

GIVEN THE SHEER number of people that the United States has attracted throughout its history, it should not be surprising that Americans have *always* been concerned about immigration. As early as 1645, the Massachusetts Bay Colony began to prohibit the entry of paupers. In 1691, the Province of New York required a new entrant to "give sufficient surety that he shall not be a burden."[4] By 1790, the United States had already welcomed over half a million immigrants, at least two-thirds of whom originated in Great Britain, and another 20 percent in Germany.

The federal government did not impose immigration restrictions for nearly a century after the founding of the United States, despite the entry of some major immigrant waves. The large-scale immigration of Germans, for instance, began after the economic and social dislocations resulting from the long Napoleonic Wars. Only 6,000 Germans entered the United States in the 1820s. During the 1840s and 1850s, however, nearly 1.4 million Germans arrived.

Ireland was the source of an equally large flow sparked mainly by the failure of the potato crop in 1845 and the subsequent Great Famine. During the 1830s, prior to the potato blight, only 171,000 Irish nationals migrated to the United States. During the 1840s and 1850s, the number rose to 1.7 million. Ireland lost a fifth of its population to the United States in two short decades.

The federal government's interest in regulating immigration was ignited by an 1875 Supreme Court ruling that invalidated state-imposed head taxes on immigrants to fund the financial burden of caring for poor entrants. Immigration policy then became the sole purview of the federal government. Congress responded by producing an ever-longer list of reasons that could be used to exclude potential migrants. In 1875, Congress prohibited the entry of prostitutes and convicts. In 1882, it suspended the immigration of Chinese laborers and added idiots, lunatics, and persons likely to become public charges to the list for good measure. By 1917, the list included persons with tuberculosis, polygamists, political radicals, and practically anyone born in Asia.

Concurrently with those busy legislative sessions, the Ellis Island–era migration was gathering force because of the technological innovation of large transatlantic steamships, which greatly reduced transportation costs; the political volatility in many countries, such as violent anti-Semitism in Russia; and the economic opportunities created by the rapid industrialization of the US economy. It is not much of an exaggeration to claim that the low-skill foreign-born workforce of the early twentieth century helped build the American manufacturing sector. Perhaps the most emblematic fact showing the immigrant's role in the rise of manufacturing is that 75 percent of the workforce at the Ford Motor Company in 1914 consisted of immigrants. Figure 3.1 illustrates the rapid increase in immigration at the beginning of the twentieth century, peaking at about 800,000 immigrants per year between 1900 and 1909.

There was also a shift in the national origin of immigrants. Traditionally, immigrants had originated in western European countries, such as Great Britain or Germany. Many of the new immigrants

FIGURE 3.1. LEGAL IMMIGRATION TO THE UNITED STATES, BY DECADE

The number for the 2010s is an extrapolation from the average number admitted between 2010 and 2013.

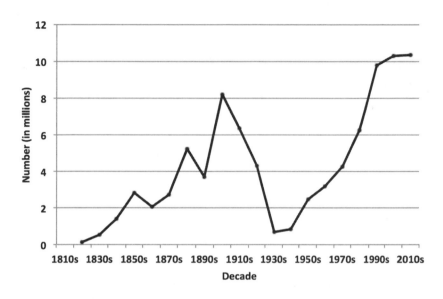

Source: US Department of Homeland Security, *Yearbook of Immigration Statistics*: 2013, table 2.

originated in Italy, Poland, and Russia. The new immigrants, it was argued, were not as intelligent or productive as the earlier waves. Francis Walker, president of the Massachusetts Institute of Technology, put it bluntly in the *Atlantic Monthly* in 1896: The new immigrants "are beaten men from beaten races; representing the worst failures in the struggle for existence. . . . They have none of the ideas and aptitudes which . . . belong to those who are descended from the tribes that met under the oak trees of old Germany to make laws and choose chieftains."[5]

Table 3.1 lists the ten largest immigrant groups residing in the United States in 1920, toward the end of the mass migration. An interesting detail is that six groups—Germans, Italians, Russians, Poles,

TABLE 3.1. THE "TOP 10" IMMIGRANT GROUPS
IN THE 1920 POPULATION

Country	Number of immigrants (in millions)	Percentage of immigrant population
1. Germany	1.7	12.1
2. Italy	1.6	11.6
3. Soviet Union	1.4	10.1
4. Poland	1.1	8.2
5. Canada	1.1	8.2
6. Great Britain	1.1	8.2
7. Ireland	1.0	7.4
8. Sweden	0.6	4.5
9. Austria	0.6	4.1
10. Mexico	0.5	3.5
All countries	13.9	—

Source: Campbell J. Gibson and Emily Lennon, "Historical Census Statistics on the Foreign-Born Population of the United States: 1850–1990," US Census Bureau, Population Division Working Paper no. 29, February 1999, table 4.

Canadians, and the British—each accounted for about 10 percent of the foreign-born population. Put differently, no single group dominated—a detail that I will come back to later, when I discuss today's mass migration.

It took a few years for the stars to align, but by the early 1920s, Congress and the president had settled on the comprehensive immigration reform that would halt the mass migration. That reform, now known as the "national origins quota system," set up a numerical limit on the number of visas that would be awarded annually (150,000), and stipulated that those visas would be allocated on the basis of national origin. As the 1924 Immigration Act states:

The annual quota of any nationality . . . shall be a number which bears the same ratio to 150,000 as the number of inhabitants in continental United States in 1920 having that national origin . . . bears to the number of inhabitants in continental United States in 1920.

For instance, 44 percent of the 1920 population was estimated to be of British ancestry, so about 44 percent of the 150,000 available visas (or 65,700) were given to Great Britain. An additional 17 percent were given to Germany and 12 percent to Ireland. In short, three countries received almost 75 percent of all available visas. The system was an obvious attempt to preserve the ethnic composition of the population, which at the time was disproportionately of British and German ancestry.

The national origins quota system remained in place until the enactment of the 1965 amendments to the immigration statutes. As part of the civil rights movement, the 1965 amendments got rid of the discrimination based on national origin and replaced it with a system that gave preference to visa applicants who already had relatives residing in the United States. Table 3.2 summarizes the main components

TABLE 3.2. COMPONENTS OF
LEGAL IMMIGRATION, 2001–2010

	Number of immigrants (in millions)
Family preference immigration	6.8
Employment-based immigration	1.6
Refugees	1.3
Diversity visas (lottery)	0.5
Other	0.3
Total	10.5

Source: US Department of Homeland Security, *Yearbook of Immigration Statistics: 2010*, table 6.

of current law, showing the number of legal immigrants admitted between 2001 and 2010 under the key provisions.

The family preference system is now responsible for about two-thirds of legal immigration. It allows the unrestricted entry of "close relatives" (parents, spouses, and minor children) of adult US citizens. Other family links are also given preference, but a numerical quota limits the number of those visas. The quotas often result in *very* long queues, with the family member waiting abroad for years before being granted the visa. For example, siblings of US citizens qualify for entry visas, but the queue (as of December 2015) was twenty-three years long for siblings of Filipino immigrants and eighteen years long for siblings of Mexican immigrants.

The 1965 legislation also allocated some visas to persons who have "exceptional ability," are "priority workers," or embody other types of desirable skills, but only about 15 percent of current immigrants use an employment-based visa. And, in fact, this number exaggerates the importance of this category because it also includes the immediate relatives of the immigrants who qualify for the employment visa.[*]

Current immigration policy recognizes that the family preference system provides an indirect way of preventing immigration from countries that have not established ethnic "roots" in the United States. After all, it is hard for foreigners to apply for family preference visas if they have no relatives residing here. As a result, we also have a "diversity visas" lottery, in which the visas are randomly distributed to lucky applicants from countries with historically low rates of immigration to the United States.

The lottery is particularly interesting because it gives a sense of the demand for entry into our country. The lottery raffles out 50,000 visas

---

[*] A vast number of programs allow temporary entry (for example, the foreign student program). Some of these temporary migrants eventually show up in Table 3.2, when they qualify for a "green card" under one of the categories of the 1965 amendments.

a year, and millions of persons apply for the opportunity to move here. In 2015, for example, the lottery received 14.9 million applications.

It is prudent to be skeptical whenever experts predict the impact of changes in immigration policy, and the enactment of the 1965 amendments provides classic examples of just how wrong the experts can be. For instance, Attorney General Robert Kennedy, when asked about the prospect of Asian immigration, assured a House subcommittee in 1964 that "5,000 immigrants could come in the first year, but we do not expect that there would be any great influx after that."[6] One year later, Attorney General Nicholas Katzenbach told the subcommittee: "If you look at the present immigration figures from Western Hemisphere countries [North and South America] there is not much pressure to come to the United States from these countries. There are in a relative sense not many people who want to come."[7]

These forecasts could not have been more wrong. They completely missed the two key demographic changes that characterize post-1965 immigration: the growing importance of Asia as a source region and the dramatic increase in immigration from Latin America. Despite the Kennedy and Katzenbach predictions, it is now widely recognized that the 1965 amendments drastically changed the number and nature of immigrants, with corresponding changes in their economic and social impact.

The immigration peak previously associated with the Ellis Island era was surpassed in the 1990s, as the economic and political forces driving the new immigration accelerated. These forces include the demand for cheap, low-skill labor in many sectors of the US economy, the very large income disparities between the United States and many developing countries, the magnet for high-skill workers created by the booming high-tech sector, and the availability of visas to persons who had long been prevented from entering the country. By the 2010s, approximately 1 million persons were entering the country legally each year.

2. ILLEGAL IMMIGRATION

ALTHOUGH THE STATUTE that regulates legal immigration to the United States has not changed in significant ways since 1965, a new development has become increasingly important and more divisive: illegal immigration.

The initial flow of undocumented immigrants began soon after the discontinuation of the Bracero Program in the 1960s, a program that allowed some Mexicans to enter the country temporarily and work in the agricultural sector. The official history of the United Farm Workers union describes the economic and political pressures that led to the birth and death of the program:

> The Bracero program, an informal arrangement between the United States and Mexican governments, became Public Law 78 in 1951. Started during World War II as a program to provide Mexican agricultural workers to growers, it continued after the war. Public Law 78 stated that no bracero—a temporary worker imported from Mexico—could replace a domestic worker. In reality this provision was rarely enforced. In fact the growers had wanted the Bracero program to continue after the war precisely in order to replace domestic workers. . . . Over time, however, farmworkers, led by Cesar Chavez, were able to call upon allies in other unions, in churches and in community groups affiliated with the growing civil rights movement, to put enough pressure on politicians to end the Bracero program by 1964.[8]

The abrupt termination of the Bracero Program represented an attempt to protect the job opportunities of agricultural workers already in the United States. The end of the program, however, did not change the "fundamentals": growers in the United States wanted to hire cheap labor, and laborers in Mexico wanted better jobs. These complementary desires were the spark that ignited the flow of undocumented immigrants. The continuation of this flow into the 1970s and 1980s led to the 1986 enactment of the Immigration Reform and Control Act (IRCA), a statute that granted amnesty to nearly 3 million persons, the vast majority originating in Mexico, and that made it illegal for employers to "knowingly hire" undocumented immigrants.

At the time that IRCA was debated, it was argued that the employer sanctions would deter undocumented immigrants. Nevertheless, many more millions arrived after IRCA than before. The fact that we have already had a major amnesty and that it did not work is partly the reason why the debate over "comprehensive immigration reform" is so contentious. It is worth noting, however, that IRCA's "failure to deter" was a feature, not a bug. The political compromise that got the law through Congress introduced a major loophole:

> Though IRCA imposed employer sanctions, it did not require employers to determine the authenticity of the documents. The loophole produced an aggressive surge in false documentation. Unauthorized workers presented counterfeit green cards, passports, driver's licenses, and other documents. And employers hired workers with these phony documents. Employers could . . . continue to hire undocumented workers.[9]

Equally important, many sectors of the US economy, not just the agricultural sector, have an insatiable appetite for cheap, low-skill workers. And this appetite is a very strong magnet to the poor and huddled masses abroad. As long as there are gains to be had, by *both* the employers and the potential migrants, and few penalties to pay, by *both* the employers and the potential migrants, the incentives remain and illegal immigration continues.

The Mexican component of illegal immigration—the component that is most controversial—may be unprecedented in terms of its size (more on that to follow), but it reflects those fundamentals. There is plenty of demand for the type of labor that Mexican immigrants can offer to profit-seeking employers, and the economic opportunities in the US labor market are far better than what Mexico offers. As economist Gordon Hanson puts it:

> For low-skilled workers in much of the world, U.S. admission policies make illegal immigration the most viable means of entering the country. . . . Given low average schooling, few Mexican citizens qualify for employment-based green cards or most types of temporary work visas. . . . Family-based immigration visas have queues that are too long and admission criteria that are too arbitrary to serve most prospective migrants who would like to work in the United States. . . . As a consequence, most Mexican immigrants enter the United States illegally.[10]

At the core of today's debate over illegal immigration lies a simple question: How many undocumented persons reside in the United States?

The Department of Homeland Security estimates the size of the undocumented population. As of January 2012, there were 11.4 million undocumented immigrants, a number that (the DHS claims) has held steady since 2006.[11] Almost 60 percent of these immigrants are from Mexico, and the next two largest groups, originating in El Salvador and Guatemala, account for an additional 11 percent. Because of the politically explosive nature of the 11.4 million statistic, it is worth looking under the hood of the calculation and figuring out exactly how DHS arrives at such a count of an elusive population.

The calculation is easy to describe. We "know" how many legal immigrants should reside in the United States at a point in time. Officials have kept good track of the number of legal immigrants admitted each year for decades (as in Figure 3.1), so we can predict how many legal immigrants should be alive and residing in the country.

At the same time, the Census Bureau periodically conducts surveys of the population and asks the respondents where they were born. The answers give us an estimate of how many foreign-born people are actually living in the country. In rough terms, the difference between the number of foreign-born persons actually living in the country and the number of legal immigrants who should be living in the country is the DHS estimate of the number of undocumented persons.*

It is easy to see one major problem with the calculation: the Census Bureau clearly misses many people whenever it goes out and tries to enumerate, and many of the people it misses are probably the undocumented immigrants who do not want to be found in the first place. To estimate the size of the undocumented population, therefore, DHS must make an assumption about the undercount rate. The official assumption is that the Census Bureau misses 10 percent of the undocumented immigrants.

I sometimes have fun when I get into a discussion of this issue by asking people what they think is the DHS assumption about the undercount rate. Frequently, the answer is "at least 30 percent." One does not need to be a full-fledged conspiracy theorist to suspect that a 10 percent undercount rate seems low. If the undercount rate were higher, of course, the official estimate of the size of the illegal population would increase correspondingly. For example, if the rate had been assumed to be 20 percent, the number of undocumented persons would rise from 11.4 to about 13 million. And if it were 30 percent, the number of undocumented persons would approach 15 million. In other words, the undercount assumption matters a lot.

So where exactly does the 10 percent assumption come from? A scavenger hunt of footnotes across various DHS reports eventually reveals the rationale:

> The estimate of net census undercount of 10% for unauthorized residents is consistent with results reported in a paper by Enrico Marcelli, "2000 Census Coverage of Foreign-born Mexicans in Los Angeles County: Implications for Demographic Analysis," pre-

---

* The difference adjusts for some return migration and for the number of foreign-born persons residing in the country temporarily.

sented at the 2000 Annual Meeting of the Population Association
of America, Atlanta, GA.[12]

Or, in plainer English, the 10 percent assumption comes from data
reported in an unpublished study that looks at the undercount rate of
Mexicans in Los Angeles County in 2000. It is doubtful that this statistic, even if it were correct in that very narrow context, provides much
information about the undercount rate for the much larger population
of undocumented immigrants today.

Given the shaky foundation for this key assumption in the DHS
calculation, it is understandable that observers seem perpetually surprised whenever a government program tries to predict the number
of undocumented immigrants that will apply for some benefit and
"unexpectedly" many more show up. As the *Sacramento Bee* reported
in April 2015: "A surge of undocumented immigrants seeking driver's
licenses has surprised the California Department of Motor Vehicles,
pouring in at twice the rate officials expected."[13]

There are good reasons for Americans to be skeptical about government pronouncements that purport to describe demographic or economic conditions in politically sensitive issues. As with our discussion
of the gains from open borders, we often acquire a new appreciation
for how to interpret "expert evidence" by looking closely at the nuts
and bolts of how we come to believe certain things about immigration.

3. THE FOREIGN-BORN POPULATION IN 2014

BECAUSE OF THE large increase in both legal and illegal immigration, 42.2 million foreigners now reside in the United States (see Table
3.3). These immigrants make up 13.3 percent of the overall population,
a fraction that is almost triple what it was back in 1970 (when it was
4.7 percent), and close to the fraction that was foreign-born during the
Ellis Island era in 1910, when it was 14.7 percent.

TABLE 3.3 THE "TOP 10" IMMIGRANT GROUPS
IN THE 2014 POPULATION

Country	Number of immigrants (in millions)	Percentage of immigrant population
1. Mexico	11.7	27.7
2. India	2.2	5.2
3. Philippines	1.9	4.6
4. China	1.9	4.5
5. El Salvador	1.3	3.1
6. Vietnam	1.3	3.1
7. Cuba	1.2	2.8
8. Korea	1.1	2.6
9. Dominican Republic	1.0	2.4
10. Guatemala	0.9	2.2
All countries	42.2	—

Source: Author's calculations using the 2014 American Community Survey.

Despite the Kennedy and Katzenbach promises, five of the top ten countries responsible for the 42 million immigrants are in Asia, and the other five are in Latin America. One single country—Mexico—accounts for 28 percent of the immigrant population. The large size of Mexican immigration is unique from a historical perspective. As we saw earlier, the two largest immigrant groups in 1920 originated in Germany and Italy, and *together* they accounted for 24 percent of the foreign-born population.

It is also useful at the outset to get a broad perspective of how the socioeconomic background of immigrants compares with that of natives. As Table 3.4 shows, the gender mix of natives and immigrants is essentially the same (49 percent are men), but immigrants are 7 years older. The popular perception that immigration is composed mainly of young men is simply incorrect. In addition, immigrants are

TABLE 3.4. CHARACTERISTICS OF IMMIGRANTS AND NATIVES, 2014

	Natives	Immigrants
Average age (in years)	37.2	44.2
Proportion male	49.3%	48.7%
Proportion living in California, Florida, New York, or Texas	29.6%	55.4%
Proportion without a high school diploma	8.0%	28.2%
Proportion with at least a college education	31.9%	29.6%
Proportion employed	72.5%	72.9%
Average annual earnings (in thousands)	$51.5	$44.6
Number of persons (in millions)	276.6	42.2

Source: Author's calculations using the 2014 American Community Survey. The statistics on education, employment, and earnings refer to the sample of persons aged twenty-five to sixty-four.

much more geographically clustered than natives. Over half of the immigrants live in the four main immigrant-receiving states, but only 30 percent of the native population lives in those states.

Finally, there are some crucial differences in skills and economic status. Immigrants and natives are equally likely to have at least a college education (about 30 percent of both groups are college graduates). However, immigrants are far more likely to lack a high school diploma; only about 8 percent of natives failed to finish high school, as compared to 28 percent of immigrants. The disproportionately large number of low-skill immigrants will be seen in later chapters to have important implications. Finally, although immigrants and natives are equally likely to hold a job, employed natives, on average, earn about 15 percent more.

The complex web of statutes, regulations, *and* unenforced laws that define real-world immigration policy creates the rules that allow only some people to enter the United States. Those rules help shape the distribution of abilities and talents that immigrants can offer, which in turn help determine the economic impact of immigration.

4

The Self-Selection of Immigrants

BRITISH PRIME MINISTER Tony Blair once quipped a core truth about immigration: "A simple way to take measure of a country is to look at how many want in . . . and how many want out."[1]

The United States has perennially been the type of place where tens of millions of foreigners want in—and 92 million, and counting, have already managed it. From the perspective of someone abroad, it is easy to see why our country is such a magnet: unrivaled opportunities for gaining wealth and the appeal of the American dream. From the American perspective, however, the lure introduces a new concern: Which types of persons is the magnet attracting?

It is fascinating to contrast the very different perceptions of who the immigrants are throughout US history. In 1753, Benjamin Franklin offered his scathing opinion of German immigrants: "Those who come hither are generally of the most ignorant Stupid Sort of their own Nation."[2] Intriguingly, Franklin's attitude was presumably based on something more than raw bigotry; he had, as a young man, published the first German-language newspaper in America, the *Philadelphische Zeitung*.

Two and a half centuries later, we are still mired in a contentious debate over immigration. Franklin's appraisal remains represented: simply change the word "German" to some other nationality referring to a developing country, and something akin to Franklin's observation resurfaces in the modern debate. We also frequently hear a different story, particularly among the political class and in the media. Immigrants are not the "most ignorant stupid sort," but rather they are ambitious, driven, and epitomize the best and the brightest that the world has to offer.

For instance, in his review of *El Norte*, a 1983 film that depicts the hardships encountered as two young Guatemalans make their way to the United States, film critic Roger Ebert observed: "So many of our immigrants are the best and the brightest. . . . One reason immigrants often seem to do well here is that they were self-selected as brave and determined." Mitt Romney echoes this sentiment when he notes: "We are the children and grandchildren and great-grandchildren of the ones who wanted a better life, the driven ones." And Barack Obama, starting from the presumption that the United States has attracted the best and the brightest in the past, argues: "If we want to keep attracting the best and the brightest from beyond our shores, we're going to have to fix our immigration system."[3]

Despite the different perspectives, the sound bites that typecast the persons attracted by the US magnet expose another core truth about immigration: not all immigrants are alike. Some groups do poorly in the United States, while other groups excel. In fact, one's gut reaction to immigration may well depend on what one believes about the process that selects the immigrants. Do they lack ability and ambition? Or are they "the best and the brightest from beyond our shores"?

Regardless of which camp one chooses to side with, the underlying idea is worth pondering: *Immigrants are self-selected.* They are not randomly chosen from the population of the sending countries.

It is far-fetched to claim that the typical immigrants from such countries as India, Mexico, and Poland has similar capabilities and will have similar economic effects. Different countries offer different opportunities to their citizens, making it inevitable that the different groups bring different things to the US economy. It is equally far-fetched to claim that the typical Mexican or Indian in the United

States is representative of the Mexican or Indian populations. The type of person who chooses to move out of a particular country probably differs dramatically across countries.

Any assessment of the impact of immigration requires that we understand what leads some persons to emigrate and others to stay behind. A valuable lesson from the existing research is that the best and the brightest flow to the country that values them the most—just as smartphones, refrigerators, and cars are shipped to the highest bidder. It should not be surprising that the US magnet attracts high-skill workers when US employers reward skills more than employers in the sending countries do. And it also should not be surprising that we miss out on attracting the best and the brightest when some other place rewards them more than we do.

The immigrant population in the United States is then composed of many different groups—groups that are self-selected in different ways and, as a result, have different talents to offer. The self-selection raises the possibility that the types of immigrants moving to the United States might not be exactly the types that the country is looking for.

Much of immigration policy can be interpreted as an attempt to refine (and perhaps to undo) what the self-selection process begets. Receiving countries do not lie back and accept the fate of being inundated by whomever the magnet attracts. Canada and Australia, for example, discourage the immigrants that so concerned Benjamin Franklin by grading visa applicants on the basis of education, occupation, and work experience. In the United States, a striking example of an attempt to undo some of the self-selection is the Immigration Act of 1917. This legislation instituted a literacy test and then listed the personal traits that would prohibit entry into the country:

All idiots, imbeciles, feeble-minded persons, epileptics, insane persons; persons who have had one or more attacks of insanity . . . ; persons of constitutional psychopathic inferiority; persons with chronic alcoholism; paupers; professional beggars; vagrants; persons afflicted with tuberculosis . . . or with a loathsome or dangerous contagious disease . . . persons who have been convicted of or admit having committed a felony or other crime or misdemeanor involving moral turpitude; polygamists . . . anarchists, or persons who believe in or advocate the overthrow by force or violence of the Government of the United States.

Despite the very long list of unwanted traits, there are limits to what such policy refinements can accomplish. If the US magnet attracts the tired, the poor, and the wretched refuse of those teeming shores, there is little that immigration policy can do, short of handing out large cash payouts, to persuade the best and the brightest to come. Policy tweaks can prevent the entry of persons who would have liked to come, but they cannot force the entry of persons who can do better elsewhere. In the end, economic and social conditions in the United States and abroad create the magnetic waves that induce *some* people to move, and all that policy restrictions can do is manipulate around the margins of this self-selected flow.

1. BARRIERS TO MIGRATION

LET ME START with a claim that some Americans might find odd: many people do not find it worthwhile to move to the United States.

There are huge income differences across countries; the typical worker in many developing countries could easily double his or her wage by moving to the industrialized First World. We would expect such income gaps to generate very large flows of migrants from poor to rich countries, and particularly to the United States. After all, who would not want a chance to live the American dream? If people were simply seeking the best economic opportunity available and if it were cheap to migrate, it is easy to imagine that many countries would have emptied out by now, as the wealth-seeking *Homo economicus* moved to whichever place was offering the best-paying job.

But most potential destinations enact policies that prevent those flows. Sometimes the policies are lax. The United States chooses to look the other way as millions of persons cross the border illegally. Other times the policies are strict. Singapore prohibits guest workers from becoming pregnant, and any woman who does is immediately expelled.

Policy restrictions, however, cannot be the only factor limiting migration to richer countries. Even when there are no such restrictions, many people *choose* not to move. This "self-censoring" suggests that, in some sense, it must be very costly to move to another place. The moving costs then overwhelm the economic benefits, persuading potential migrants to stay put.

All the available evidence indicates that moving costs are an important barrier to migration. In 2010, for instance, a construction worker in his thirties earned $23,000 in Puerto Rico and $43,000 in the continental United States. The income of such a Puerto Rican worker, therefore, would increase by $20,000 annually if he or she were to move to the mainland, and the gain would still be very large, even if adjusted for differences in the cost of living. Added up over two or three decades, a move could easily generate more than a quarter-million-dollar lifetime gain.

No legal restrictions exist to prevent a Puerto Rican from moving here; Puerto Ricans are US citizens by birth. All it takes is a one-way plane ticket that costs a fraction of a week's salary. The worker can board the plane in San Juan and disembark in Miami or New York three or four hours later, where family, friends, and compatriots stand ready to ease the transition into the new environment.

Many Puerto Ricans have, in fact, made this journey. But, more intriguingly, two-thirds of Puerto Ricans *have chosen not to move*, leaving a substantial fortune unclaimed. By staying put, the nonmovers are indicating that the moving costs—as *they* perceive them—exceed $250,000.

A similarly illuminating example involves the move from East Germany to West Germany in the early years of the Cold War.

East Germany was a particularly repressive totalitarian state, and its economy lagged behind that of the booming West. It would seem that most people living in East Germany at the time would have found few reasons to stay there.

Prior to the building of the Berlin Wall on August 13, 1961, all it took for an East Berliner to escape was to board a suburban train or a subway (the S-Bahn or U-Bahn). Those trains ran unobstructed from one side of Berlin to the other. And indeed, there was a lot of short-term commuting between the two worlds: "East Berliners streamed to the cinema, theatres and Berlin Philharmonic concerts in West Berlin. . . . They scraped together their hard-earned wages . . . to buy western clothing, cosmetics and a thousand other items unavailable in the east. . . . At the same time, West Berliners often made up a third of the audience at East Berlin's two opera houses and Bertolt Brecht's famed Berliner Ensemble theatre."[4]

The easy "commute" meant that any would-be refugee from the communist regime could end up in free and vibrant West Berlin in minutes. And in fact, many East Germans jumped at the opportunity. A declassified CIA memo dated August 10, 1961, just three days before the Berlin Wall was built, describes conditions on the ground:

West Germany has registered more than 2,600,000 refugees from East Germany since 1949. . . . Published East German statistics acknowledge a steady slow decline of the total population from 19,066,000 in 1948 to approximately 17,200,000 at the end of last year. . . . So far this year the volume of refugees is the highest since 1953. The high proportion of professionals, engineers, and intellectuals has been of particular concern to the [East German] regime. . . . In recent weeks, however, an additional element seems to have been the developing crisis over West Berlin, which has led to widespread fear not only of war but also that chances for escape might soon disappear. . . . *There is some evidence that the regime is considering harsher measures to reduce the flow.*[5]

The fact that West Germany imported tens of thousands of guest workers at the time indicates that jobs were plentiful. Nevertheless, although
millions of East Germans took advantage of the circumstances, millions
more did not. The emigration rate was less than 15 percent, again suggesting the presence of some powerful force holding back the vast majority. We do not know exactly what that force was, but the implication that
there is a sizable barrier or "cost" to moving is inescapable.

These examples may seem contrived, but far more sophisticated
studies of the migration decision reach the same conclusion.[6] Regardless of whether the move is across countries, across states, or across
industries, it seems ridiculously expensive to move. Average moving
costs are often estimated to be about ten times a worker's annual salary. In other words, migration costs should be measured in hundreds
of thousands of dollars, rather than just a few thousand.

What exactly is the nature of these very high costs? They do not
represent the cost of moving the family and household goods to a new
location. Instead, they suggest that the potential migrant attaches a
very high psychological value to the social, cultural, and physical ame-
nities associated with remaining where he or she was born, including
family, friends, and familiarity with old surroundings. It then takes
a very large improvement in living conditions to justify the decision
to move. As a result, many people do not find it in their best interest
to move, and those who do self-select themselves to be emigrants are
likely to be quite unrepresentative of the population at large.

2. TRENDS IN THE ENTRY WAGE

BECAUSE THE IMMIGRANTS who reach the United States represent a
small subset of the population of potential migrants, it should not be
surprising that the kind of person who chooses to come differs across
sending countries and over time. A question that often surfaces in the
immigration debate is this: Are the immigrants coming today as economically valuable as those who used to come? The interest in this

question is not surprising. The economic impact of immigration obviously depends on who the immigrants are.

A simple way of measuring the economic potential of new immigrants is to look at the wage they command at the time they enter the country. The entry wage summarizes the value of all the skills that the new immigrant brings, including education, work experience, and English-language fluency. Therefore, trends in the entry wage provide information about trends in the productivity of the immigrant population.

The census data available since 1960 let us examine the trend in the entry wage. In each census, we can calculate the wage gap between native workers and the immigrants who entered the country in the five-year period prior to the census. Note that these data include all foreign-born persons, legal and undocumented, enumerated by the Census Bureau. As Figure 4.1 shows, the historical trend in the entry wage is striking.[*]

The newest entrants in 1960 earned 11 percent less than natives. By 1990, the newest entrants had a 28 percent wage disadvantage. It seems that the skills of successive immigrant waves—relative to those of natives—declined dramatically during that period. The entry wage has stabilized since 1990; newly arrived immigrants in 2010 still earned about 28 percent less than natives. As I noted earlier, my initial interest in immigration research was sparked precisely by the notion that these types of productivity differences might exist across immigrant waves.

The decline in the entry wage of immigrants is irrefutable. But what does it mean? One obvious answer is that it does not really reflect a drop in immigrant productivity at all, but rather a change in the US labor market. A substantial decline in blue-collar employment opportunities has made it much more difficult for low-skill workers to find and hold well-paying jobs. In addition, income inequality has widened, with economic conditions for those at the bottom worsening considerably. Because immigrants, on average, are less skilled than

---

[*] In all the figures of Chapter 4, the age-adjusted differences between immigrants and natives are calculated in the sample of working men aged twenty-five to sixty-four who are not enrolled in school.

FIGURE 4.1. THE ENTRY WAGE OF IMMIGRANTS, 1960–2010

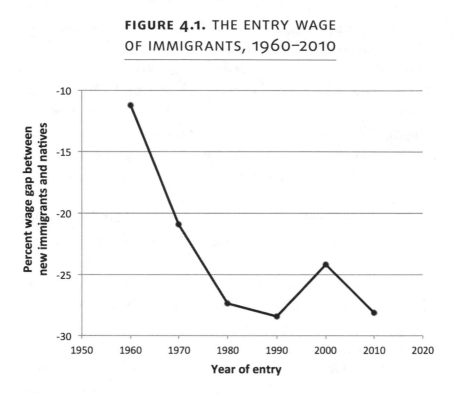

Source: Author's calculations from the 1960–2000 decennial census and the pooled 2009–2011 American Community Surveys.

natives, the decline in the entry wage could be reflecting the changing economic conditions rather than a plunge in immigrant productivity.

There is certainly some truth to this argument, but it cannot by itself explain the decline in the entry wage.[7] It is easy to see this by looking at the comparable trend in an *actual* measure of skills: the education of new immigrants (Figure 4.2). There was also a decline in their education relative to that of natives. In 1960, the two groups had essentially the same education. By 1990, the new immigrants had, on average, almost two fewer years of schooling.

Instead of reflecting deteriorating economic conditions for low-skill workers, the decline in the entry wage is connected with mainly the changing national origin of the immigrant population (away from

FIGURE 4.2. LEVEL OF EDUCATION OF NEW IMMIGRANTS COMPARED TO NATIVES, 1960–2010

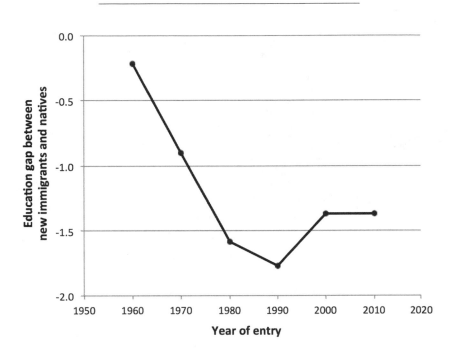

Source: Author's calculations using the 1960–2000 decennial census and the pooled 2009–2011 American Community Surveys.

Europe and toward developing countries)—a shift put in motion by the 1965 amendments. There are enormous differences in the economic performance of immigrants born in different places. Figure 4.3 shows the variation among the twenty largest groups. New immigrants from the Dominican Republic and Mexico earned about 50 percent less than natives, while those from Germany and Canada earned about 70 percent more than natives. It would not be too much of an exaggeration to claim that the best single predictor of an immigrant's economic performance in the United States is his or her country of origin.

Even the most superficial look at the variation suggests that immigrants from developing countries earn far less than those from industrialized economies (although there are exceptions, such as India).

FIGURE 4.3. VARIATION IN ENTRY WAGES AMONG IMMIGRANT GROUPS, 2010

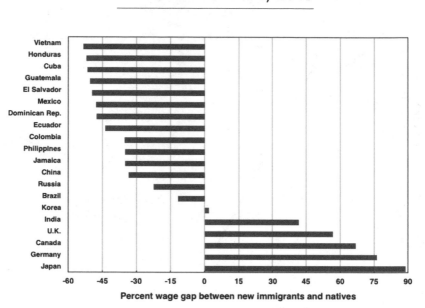

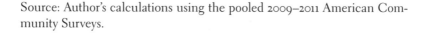

Source: Author's calculations using the pooled 2009–2011 American Community Surveys.

In 1997, the National Academy of Sciences (NAS) published the conclusions of its review of the economic impact of immigration. The report was unequivocal when noting the association between the economic status of the average immigrant and national origin:[*]

> The relative decline in the economic status of both male and female immigrants can be attributed to a single factor—the changing national origin mix of the immigrant flow. If that mix had not changed in the past few decades, we would not have seen much change in the relative wage of immigrants.[8]

---

[*] Full disclosure: I was a member of the National Academy panel that prepared the report.

The link between immigrant economic performance and national origin raises unpleasant questions. It places the sensitive issues of race and ethnicity right at the center of the debate, and forces us to ask why national origin is such an important determinant of economic outcomes.

3. WHY DOES NATIONAL ORIGIN MATTER?

MOST OF US know that different immigrant groups experience very different outcomes in the US labor market. But *why* do immigrants from Mexico or the Dominican Republic earn far less than immigrants from Germany or Canada? It turns out that a small number of fundamentals account for the bulk of these differences.

Self-Selection

As I have emphasized, immigrants are not randomly chosen from the population of the sending countries. It is hard to come up with a better example demonstrating just how unrepresentative immigrants are than that of the typical Indian immigrant compared with the typical Indian left behind. The average person in India has less than six years of schooling, but over 70 percent of Indian immigrants in the United States have a college or graduate degree.

There has been an enduring interest in how immigrants are self-selected, and it is customary to pick one of two extremes when describing the selection. Either immigrants are the best and the brightest that the sending countries have to offer, and we benefit accordingly. Or the United States attracts the tired and the poor, and the country bears the corresponding costs.

I find these types of ideologically motivated assumptions and platitudes thoroughly unconvincing. As my interest in immigration economics began to deepen in the mid-1980s, it became obvious that the decline in the entry wage of immigrants—and the fact that this decline seemed to be related to the changing national origin of the incoming workers—required that we answer a key question: What factors motivate some persons in the sending country to stay and other persons to move?

A sensible way of thinking about the migration decision yields a rule of thumb that does a good job of predicting who will emigrate.[9] In particular, suppose the migration decision is motivated by better income opportunities abroad: a better job and a better life for the migrant and family. One can then imagine each potential migrant making a straightforward calculation, comparing the value of the income opportunities if he stays with the value of the opportunities if he moves. As long as the gain from migrating exceeds the moving costs, the person moves.

Let's zoom in on a potential migrant living in a country where skills are not well compensated, so that persons who are highly skilled do not earn much more than persons who have few skills. This situation is common in some European countries, such as Denmark or Sweden, where the welfare state and other social policies equalize the income distribution—taxing the highly skilled and subsidizing the less skilled. Many of these countries also have institutions, such as strong labor unions, that further cushion the earnings of low-skill workers. It is then obvious that the workers who have the most to gain by moving to the United States are the workers with above-average skills. Those are the workers who pay the penalty for living in a place where the payoff for being highly skilled is low. The emigrants from such a country are "positively selected" from the population, and the United States would presumably benefit from this brain drain.

At the other extreme, imagine a potential migrant living in a country where skills are very well compensated. The payoff for being skilled is large in some developing countries, such as Honduras or Haiti. And those high returns often account for the substantial income inequality observed in those countries, where the skilled earn far more than the unskilled. High-skill workers have little incentive to leave, while the less skilled, if they can afford it, will grab the first opportunity to move. The typical emigrant from such countries would be "negatively selected," and would be less skilled than the people who remain behind.

Put simply, skills flow to those places that offer the highest reward for them. The rule of thumb for immigrant selection is straightforward: the United States attracts high-skill workers from countries with egalitarian income distributions (those countries where high-skill workers do not do so well), and low-skill workers from countries with a lot of income inequality (those countries where low-skill workers do very poorly).

As Figure 4.4 shows, immigrants originating in countries where there is substantial income inequality, such as Colombia, Honduras, or Haiti, indeed earn less than immigrants originating in countries where there is much less inequality, such as India, Canada, or Austria. This relation between entry wages and inequality persists even if we compare immigrants from countries that have similar levels of economic development. In short, part of the disparity in immigrant performance arises because different types of persons choose to leave different countries.

The self-selection of immigrants raises the possibility of a mismatch between the type of worker that a receiving country "needs"

FIGURE 4.4. ENTRY WAGE AND INCOME INEQUALITY, 2010

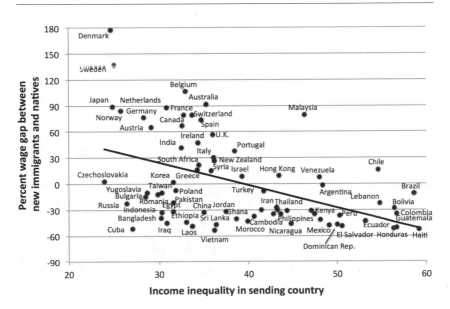

Source: Author's calculations using the pooled 2009–2011 American Community Surveys.

and the type that chooses to move there. The market for workers with advanced degrees in the biological sciences illustrates this point. Although there are widespread reports of shortages of such scientists in the United States, economist Paula Stephan, who has conducted many studies of high-skill labor markets, dismisses those claims:

> Shortages are often predicted by groups who have a vested interest in attracting more students to graduate school and into careers in science and engineering. . . . Most of the assertions come from four groups: universities and professional associations, government agencies, firms that hire scientists and engineers, and immigration lawyers. All have a considerable amount to gain by an increase in supply: universities, for example, in terms of students (and lab workers); companies in terms of the lower wages associated with an increase in supply.[10]

Instead of a shortage, she notes, "the number of PhDs in the life sciences had grown substantially in recent years but the job market opportunities for young life scientists had not kept pace."[11] The imbalance between supply and demand by the 1990s was so large that the National Research Council recommended that "there be no further expansion in the size of existing graduate-education programs in the life sciences and no development of new programs."[12]

Stephan estimates that a native student would earn about $1 million more over the lifetime by going to business school and getting an MBA than by acquiring a doctoral degree in the life sciences. These large wage gaps provide a very strong market signal, channeling bright American students into sectors where job opportunities are more plentiful. The market signal, however, may not stop the flow of foreigners into the life sciences. After all, it could be that the sending country rewards that type of highly specialized training *even less*. In fact, the fraction of life science doctorates awarded to foreign students tripled between 1980 and 2012, from about 10 to 30 percent. Because of this continued inflow, conducting this type of research could eventually become an even lower-paid occupation employing mainly immigrants, and creating the common perception that immigrants do jobs that natives don't want to do.

The discussion of immigrant self-selection becomes particularly controversial when we think about it in the context of Mexican immigration. When Donald Trump announced his presidential bid in June 2015, he made some comments that resulted in a political firestorm. Among the least incendiary of those comments was this statement: "When Mexico sends its people, they're not sending their best. . . . They're sending people that have lots of problems."[3]

Despite the subject's sensitive nature, economists have been examining the skills of Mexican immigrants for nearly three decades. A comparison of the rewards for skill in Mexico and the United States suggests that the migrant flow should be negatively selected. College graduates in Mexico earn twice as much as high school graduates, far more than the payoff for a college education in the United States. Because the economic well-being of the most educated Mexicans would not be particularly improved by their moving to the United States, immigrants from Mexico should tend to have below-average skills.

An important study by Daniel Chiquiar and Gordon Hanson developed an empirical approach for determining the selection that actually takes place.[14] They compared the education of Mexican "stayers" enumerated by the Mexican census with the education of Mexican immigrants enumerated by the US census. Surprisingly, this comparison suggested that Mexican immigrants in the United States were among neither the most educated nor the least educated persons in the Mexican population. Instead, the immigrants came from the middle of the Mexican education distribution.

One obvious problem with this comparison is that the US census does not enumerate all Mexican immigrants. Many Mexicans entered the country illegally, and the census misses many undocumented persons. As a result, the comparison of stayers in the Mexican census with the immigrants enumerated by the US census overlooks the large number of low-skill, undocumented immigrants who are living in the shadows.

Subsequent research improved on the Chiquiar-Hanson approach by discarding the US census data altogether and focusing on surveys from Mexico that report the economic status of persons *prior* to their becoming migrants. This research indicates that the Mexicans who choose to move earn about 30 percent less than the average stayer.[15] Because earnings are a much more encompassing measure of skills than is education, the recent evidence confirms that Mexican immigrants are indeed disproportionately drawn from the low-skill workforce.

It is important to emphasize that this evidence does *not* imply that Mexican immigrants lack drive and motivation. After all, the migrants' poor performance in Mexico could have been the result of social, cultural, and economic barriers that they faced in developing their full potential—barriers that might perhaps disappear after they moved to the United States.

In sum, the immigrant population is composed of persons who find that the United States offers a better price for whatever it is they have to offer. Broad stereotypes about immigrants being the best and the brightest (or not!) are wrong. Sometimes immigrants represent a brain drain, and sometimes they do not. And ideological blinders—as formidable as they are—cannot obscure *that* core truth about immigration.

Economic Development

Even putting aside the issue of self-selection, the variation in entry wages across immigrant groups suggests that immigrants who originate in richer countries tend to do better. As Figure 4.5 shows, immigrants from rich countries earn far more than those from poor countries.

Immigrants from richer countries do better partly because they have the opportunity to acquire more education prior to their move. A typical adult has completed five years of school in Haiti, nine years

FIGURE 4.5. ENTRY WAGE AND ECONOMIC DEVELOPMENT, 2010

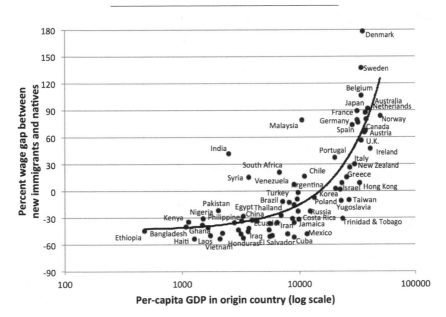

Source: Author's calculations using the pooled 2009–2011 American Community Surveys.

in Mexico, ten years in Chile, and over twelve years in Israel or Canada. The variation in earnings across immigrant groups in the United States is bound to reflect the variation that exists in educational opportunities across countries.

However, the reason that originating in a rich country matters is not just that people born in those countries are better educated. Even among immigrants who have the same education, those who come from richer countries still do better. It may be that the skills acquired in industrialized economies tend to be equally useful in other industrialized economies, while the skills acquired in developing countries are less useful in an industrialized setting.[16] Put differently, a larger fraction of the skills acquired in a rich country "survive" the move to the United States, further improving the economic performance of those immigrants.

Undocumented Status

Another potential reason for the huge wage differences across immigrant groups is that some groups have many undocumented workers. The undocumented have a harder time searching for better job opportunities because doing so increases the chance of detection and deportation. The inability to cast a wider net in finding a job, as well as the exploitation these workers may suffer because of their status, limits the undocumented immigrant's potential. Obviously, the average economic performance of an immigrant group will lag behind if there are many undocumented workers in that group.

Undocumented workers do, in fact, make up a large fraction of some of the groups that have low entry wages (see Table 4.1). The Department of Homeland Security estimates that, in 2012, 6.7 million Mexicans were undocumented, and these undocumented persons accounted for 55 percent of the Mexican-born population in the United States. Similarly, nearly 400,000 Hondurans were undocumented, and they made up almost two-thirds of the Honduran population in the United States.

TABLE 4.1. UNDOCUMENTED IMMIGRATION, 2012

Country of origin	Number of undocumented immigrants	Percentage of immigrant group that is undocumented
Mexico	6,720,000	55.3
El Salvador	690,000	52.1
Guatemala	560,000	59.8
Honduras	360,000	63.0
Philippines	310,000	16.4
All countries	11,430,000	27.3

Source: Bryan Baker and Nancy Rytina, "Estimates of the Unauthorized Immigrant Population Residing in the United States: January 2012" (US Department of Homeland Security, March 2013), 5; and author's calculations using the 2012 American Community Survey.

Given these magnitudes, perhaps a big chunk of the wage disadvantage of Mexicans or Hondurans would vanish if the undocumented immigrants were given work permits and were free to search for better jobs and escape exploitation by unscrupulous employers.

Despite the plausibility of this argument, the available evidence does not support it. A number of studies have examined what happened to the earnings of the workers who received amnesty in 1986 as part of IRCA. Nearly 3 million undocumented immigrants were granted amnesty at the time, and surveys tracked those immigrants as they received their legal working papers. The wage of the newly legalized men rose by 6–9 percent between 1989 and 1992.[7] Clearly, legalization effects of this magnitude cannot possibly account for the wage disadvantage experienced by such immigrant groups as the Mexicans or Hondurans—groups that earn 50 percent less than natives.

Discrimination

Finally, I have skirted the issue of labor market discrimination, even though many observers instinctively gravitate toward a discrimination-based explanation whenever they see a difference between blacks and whites or men and women. Remarkably, the many studies that examine wage differences across immigrant groups have shied away from empha sizing discrimination as an important source of those differences. The reason is clear: it is doubtful that discrimination can explain the sizable disadvantage of the worst-performing immigrant groups.

To begin with, some of the immigrant groups that would typically be classified as "minority" or as "persons of color" earn at least as much as natives do; newly arrived Korean immigrants earn the same, while Indian immigrants earn 40 percent more. Even after adjusting for the very high education level of many Asian immigrants, some of those groups continue to outperform white workers. A 2014 Department of Labor study concludes:

Indian, Japanese, and Chinese Americans have the highest wages, making 32, 24, and 13 percent more than whites respectively. . . .

But if we compare individuals with the same level of education, these raw wage gaps shrink dramatically. The gaps for Indian, Japanese, and Chinese workers fall to 10, 8, and 1 percent, respectively.[18]

At the other extreme, much of the available evidence suggests that the very low earnings of the most disadvantaged groups, particularly Mexican immigrants, can be traced to their low educational attainment. In 2010, the average native worker had more than thirteen years of schooling, as compared to only nine years for Mexican immigrants. Because an additional year of education can increase earnings by as much as 10 percent, it is easy to see that the differences in education will generate correspondingly large differences in earnings. In fact, the 50 percent wage gap between natives and Mexicans would drop to about 15 percent if we simply compared workers with the same education and English-language proficiency.

A well-known study of the earnings of US-born persons of Mexican ancestry by economist Stephen Trejo emphasizes the different sources of the Mexican-white and black-white wage gaps:

> Mexican Americans earn low wages primarily because they possess less human capital than other workers, not because they receive smaller labor market rewards for their skills. . . . For Mexicans, more than three-quarters of the wage gap is attributable to their relative youth, English language deficiencies, and especially their lower educational attainment. By contrast, these variables explain less than a third of the black-white wage gap.[19]

In other words, even though differences in skills do not explain much of the black-white wage gap, leading to the conclusion that much of that gap reflects the pernicious effects of racial discrimination, a large portion of the Mexican-white wage gap disappears once we compare similarly educated workers.

Although the problems faced by disadvantaged minority groups are often attributed to discriminatory forces operating at many levels of American society, this explanation is not credible when it comes to immigrants. The evidence instead points in a different direction. Some immigrant groups earn less simply because they are less skilled. Sometimes it is low-skill workers who find it most beneficial to move to the United States, and the capabilities they bring may not be so easily transferable to the American setting.

5

Economic Assimilation

W E HAVE SEEN the trends in the skills that immigrants bring with them to the United States, and the large differences among immigrant groups. But those capabilities and talents might not remain stagnant for long. The skills that immigrants offer to US employers will likely change as they exploit the many new opportunities that are now available. But does the economic well-being of immigrants improve significantly over time? Put simply, do immigrants assimilate?

This seems to be the type of question that could be answered conclusively by looking at data and documenting whether the economic outcomes of immigrants and natives become more similar over time. The answer, however, is neither as straightforward nor as unequivocal as the ideological poles in the immigration debate make it out to be. The reality is far more nuanced: some immigrants assimilate quickly, and some do not; assimilation seems to be a common experience at some points in American history, and a far less common one at other points. In short, there is a lot of variation in the rate at which different groups assimilate, and this disparity raises a much more important question: Which factors help or hinder the assimilation process?

Most discussions of assimilation presume that it is a desirable outcome—at least from the point of view of the United States. It seems silly to even ponder whether we should think of assimilation as a positive development, but the question is not as far-fetched as it seems. For instance, one often-heard argument in favor of immigration is that immigrants do jobs that natives don't want to do. If the gains from immigration derive from this division of labor, it is far from clear that assimilation benefits natives. After all, if immigrants eventually become just like us, who will do the jobs that we do not want to do?

The problem with the argument that the assimilation of immigrants might not be so beneficial for natives is that it views assimilation from a very myopic perspective of economic costs and benefits. The concept of economic assimilation is far narrower than the cultural and social integration that really lies at the core of the debate. Assimilation is not simply, and perhaps even mainly, an economic phenomenon. However, economic assimilation is tied to—and probably goes together with—other forms of integration.

Although assimilation may mean that the immigrants lose some cultural traditions, the gains for the United States could be substantial. The immigration debate in Europe, for example, revolves around the perceived presence of large unassimilated groups in their society. As a team of European economists note: "It is widely believed that many European countries have a serious problem with the integration of immigrants and their children. . . . Poor economic success may lead to social and economic exclusion of immigrants and their descendants, which in turn may lead to social unrest, with riots and terrorism as extreme manifestations (as experienced by the U.K. and France at various times)."[1]

In 2004, Samuel Huntington, perhaps the pre-eminent political scientist of his generation, published a controversial essay entitled *The Hispanic Challenge*. This essay crystallized the argument that assimilation for new immigrants, and particularly for Hispanic immigrants, was not proceeding at the historical pace. Huntington was characteristically blunt:

> In the past, immigrants originated overseas and often overcame severe obstacles and hardships to reach the United States. They came

from many different countries, spoke different languages, and came
legally. Their flow fluctuated over time. They dispersed into many
enclaves in rural areas and major cities. . . . On all these dimensions,
Mexican immigration is fundamentally different. These differences
combine to make the assimilation of Mexicans into U.S. culture and
society much more difficult than it was for previous immigrants.[2]

Huntington, in fact, was worried not only about the Mexican component of Hispanic immigration, which is disproportionately low-skill.
Regarding the settlement of Cubans in Miami, he wrote:

> "In Miami there is no pressure to be American," one Cuban-born
> sociologist observed. "People can make a living perfectly well in an
> enclave that speaks Spanish." By 1999, the heads of Miami's larg-
> est bank, largest real estate development company, and largest law
> firm were all Cuban-born or of Cuban descent. . . . The Cuban
> and Hispanic dominance of Miami left Anglos (as well as blacks)
> as outside minorities that could often be ignored.[3]

Huntington identified a number of factors that he believed were
hampering the assimilation of Hispanics: their sheer number, their
extreme geographic clustering, and the tenacious persistence of the
flow. Combined, he argued, these factors created an environment
where the typical immigrant barely benefits from assimilation, and
hence little assimilation occurs.

Huntington's conclusions did not go unchallenged. Many other
observers concluded that there was little to worry about because all
immigrants, including Hispanic immigrants, were assimilating just
fine. *New York Times* columnist David Brooks, for example, wrote:

> Huntington marshals a body of evidence to support his claims.
> But the most persuasive evidence is against him. . . . Latinos are
> quite adept at climbing out of poverty. Sixty-eight percent of those
> who have been in this country 30 years own their own homes. . . .

When they have children, they tend to lose touch with their Mexican villages and sink roots here.[4]

The optimistic appraisal was pounded in countless reports and editorials in the past few years, as the debate over immigration took center stage in the political arena. Regardless of their location in the ideological spectrum, the commentators painted a mostly optimistic picture. From the Manhattan Institute:

> Immigrants of the past quarter-century have assimilated more rapidly than their counterparts of a century ago, even though they are more distinct from the native population upon arrival.[5]

And from the Center for American Progress:

> Claims that immigrants are stuck at the bottom of the ladder are due simply to the newness of immigrants and the lack of time for assimilation to occur. Given time, the evidence plainly shows that our immigrants today are growing ever more successful and becoming part and parcel of the fabric of our nation.[6]

Because the acquisition of skills and the evolution of earnings can be objectively measured, the process of economic assimilation is far easier to document than is integration along other dimensions. The main lesson from the evidence is obvious, though often ignored: immigrants, like the rest of us, respond to incentives. If immigrants find it profitable to assimilate, they will take actions that facilitate the assimilation process. If immigrants find it worthwhile to remain a group apart, that, too, can happen. It should not be surprising that assimilation differs across national origins and fluctuates over time as economic, cultural, and political conditions change.

Despite what advocates want to hear, the correct answer to the question "Do immigrants assimilate?" is not a simple yes or no. It is, instead, it depends. And it depends on the factors, including skill level, size of the ethnic group, and geographic clustering, that common sense suggests will speed up or slow down the assimilation process.

1. MEASURING ASSIMILATION

IF WE COULD take a bird's-eye snapshot of how immigrants are performing in the United States *today*, we would surely find large differences in outcomes between the immigrants who have just arrived and those who arrived many years ago. The new arrivals would undoubtedly be worse off: they would earn less; they would be less likely to speak English; they would be less likely to own their homes.

In fact, whenever we carry out these point-in-time comparisons, we find that the new arrivals tend to do far worse than natives, while the longtime immigrants sometimes do at least as well as natives and sometimes do far better. In 2010, for example, immigrant men who had been in the country fewer than five years earned almost 30 percent less than natives, while immigrants who had arrived in the early 1970s earned only 5 percent less.

In 1978, Barry Chiswick published a study that took the bird's-eye view of the 1970 census and documented for the first time the strong link between immigrant earnings and years since arrival. Chiswick employed the concept of economic assimilation—the narrowing of differences between immigrants and natives—to offer an intuitive and influential interpretation of why new arrivals earned less than earlier arrivals.

The story goes as follows: A brand-new immigrant lacks the skills required to perform well in his new home. He is not fluent in the English language, the skills he brought may not be valued by US employers, he does not know which jobs are best or where they are located, and he may be unfamiliar with how the US labor market works. Over time, the immigrant acquires a new set of skills—learning the language, changing occupations, and moving to towns that offer better opportunities. Economic assimilation ensues as immigrant earnings catch up with those of natives.

Arnold Schwarzenegger's acquisition of skills after migrating to the United States neatly illustrates what economic assimilation is all about. He recalls how he would write specific goals on index cards: "get twelve more units in college"; "gain five pounds of solid muscle weight"; "find an apartment building to buy and move into." Schwarzenegger explains how he proceeded to achieve some of those goals:

> Immigration status was one of the obstacles I had to work around putting myself through college. I had a work visa, not a student visa, so I could only go part-time. I could never take more than two classes at once in any school, so I had to jump all over. In addition to Santa Monica College, I went to West Los Angeles College and took extension courses at the University of California at Los Angeles. I realized this would be a problem if I wanted to earn a degree, because I'd have to link all those credits to make them all count. But a degree wasn't my objective; *I only needed to study as much as I could in my available time and learn how Americans did business.*[7]

In the same vein, Jose Antonio Vargas, a Pulitzer Prize–winning journalist from the Philippines who entered the United States as an undocumented immigrant, describes the work he put into learning to speak and write English:

> Though I learned English in the Philippines, I wanted to lose my accent. During high school, I spent hours at a time watching television (especially "Frasier," "Home Improvement" and reruns of "The Golden Girls") and movies (from "Goodfellas" to "Anne of Green Gables"), pausing the VHS to try to copy how various characters enunciated their words. At the local library, I read magazines, books and newspapers—anything to learn how to write better.[8]

As an economist would phrase it, Schwarzenegger and Vargas were "investing in human capital." They devoted a lot of time and effort, and gave up many other activities, to improve the qualifications they could offer to the US economy.

The influence of Chiswick's "assimilationist" interpretation of why earlier immigrants do better than more recent arrivals persists to this day. An editorial published in the *Wall Street Journal* in 2013 proclaimed: "Latino immigrants who have been in the U.S. for three decades or more are also more likely than recent arrivals to own a home, live in a family with an income above the federal poverty line and marry outside of their ethnic group—all common measures of assimilation."[9]

It is certainly tempting to interpret the gap between earlier and new arrivals as assimilation, but this temptation often leads down the wrong path. There is, after all, another obvious reason why the most recent immigrants may not perform as well as the earlier ones: perhaps they are different groups of people. As I noted earlier, my interest in the economics of immigration was sparked precisely by this issue: How exactly should one interpret the fact that immigrants who have been in the country a long time earn more than those who have been in the country a short time?

We have already seen the dramatic changes in the skills that immigrants have brought with them over the past few decades. The immigrants who arrived in the 1950s and 1960s had high wages at the time of entry, but the entry wage began to decline with the waves that entered in the 1970s and 1980s. Given this trend, it is inevitable that at any point in time, the new arrivals will not do as well as the old, but this says nothing about assimilation. It simply indicates that the new and the old arrivals are different types of workers, with the new arrivals being less productive.

My initial study in the economics of immigration, published in 1985, argued that the point-in-time comparison might not measure assimilation correctly.[10] I proposed that we needed to *track* specific waves of immigrants over time to see how their earnings had grown as they accumulated experience in the United States.

For example, we could track a group of young immigrants who arrived in the late 1960s across the decades. The 1970 census would report their entry wage, while the 1980 census would report their wage ten years later. The tracking would help us see whether the economic performance of this specific group was catching up to that of young natives over the same period. It turned out that this tracking exercise implied far less assimilation than was suggested by the point-in-time snapshot.

I presented a draft of that study at the 1984 Summer Institute run by the National Bureau of Economic Research (NBER) in Cambridge, Massachusetts—a sort of annual summer camp for economists. The paper was very well received, almost surely because of its methodological contribution. Specifically, it showed how the commonsense assimilationist interpretation of an interesting fact—recent arrivals earn less than earlier arrivals—could be completely wrong, and it provided a way for correctly measuring assimilation.

Edward Lazear, who would head the Council of Economic Advisers in the George W. Bush administration two decades later, was one of the seminar participants. At the time, he was editor of the *Journal of Labor Economics*, a newly established academic journal out of the University of Chicago. He approached me immediately after the presentation and asked me something to the effect of: "What are you doing with the paper?" I told him that I had submitted it to *his* journal for consideration a few months earlier and was still waiting for a response about whether the journal's editorial board liked it enough to publish it. He said: "It's accepted." I know that I am not the only academic who wishes that the process of getting a paper published was this easy all the time.

The reaction at countless other presentations that I gave at the time was similar. I do not recall much discussion of the policy implications of my findings—whatever they happen to be. But I do recall much interest in the discovery that there was a difficult methodological issue that needed to be addressed in measuring the rate of assimilation.

I wish I was wrong about this, but if an equivalent paper were to make the rounds today, the contribution would no longer be judged solely on what it teaches us about how exactly one should go about doing this or that. Instead, the findings would be put through an ideological filter, and the reception in the highly politicized immigration community would very much depend on how well the results fit a preconceived narrative.

The immigration surge in the United States is now several decades old, and the available census data enable us to track the performance of specific waves for a much longer period. For example, we can track the young immigrants who arrived in the late 1960s into the 2000 and 2010 censuses, to see how the group was performing thirty or forty years later.

The trends in assimilation implied by this approach are very informative. Figure 5.1 shows the wage growth experienced by specific immigrant waves over time—relative to the growth of comparably aged natives.* In short, it illustrates how fast the earnings of immigrants are catching up to the earnings of natives. Evidently, the economic performance of the immigrants who arrived before 1980 improved dramatically. Their earnings grew by about 10 percentage points in the first decade, and by 15–20 percentage points after thirty years.[11]

The assimilation outlook, however, is far less optimistic for the more recent waves. The earnings of the immigrants who arrived in the late 1980s grew by only 5 percentage points in the first ten years and did not improve after that. Most disturbing, the earnings of the immigrants who arrived in the late 1990s did not grow at all in the first decade. There seems to have been a dramatic *slowdown* in economic assimilation.

2. IS THE SLOWDOWN REAL?

THERE ARE TWO main explanations for the assimilation slowdown documented in Figure 5.1. The first is that the tracking of an immigrant wave from census to census does not capture the catch-up process correctly. There may be things going on in the economy that conceal the assimilation that is actually taking place. The deteriorating conditions

---

* In Figures 5.1 and 5.2, the immigrant-native age-adjusted wage differences are calculated in a sample of working men aged twenty-five to sixty-four who are not enrolled in school.

FIGURE 5.1. TRENDS IN ASSIMILATION, 1940–2010

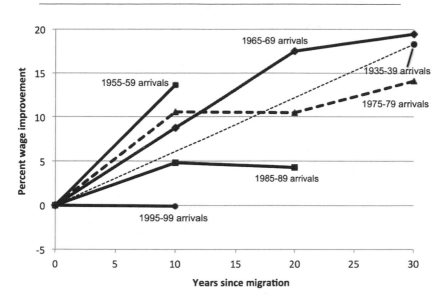

Source: Author's calculations using the 1940–2000 decennial censuses and the pooled 2009–2011 American Community Surveys.

facing low-skill workers surely made it harder for the typical immigrant to keep up, let alone catch up, with natives. The second explanation is more troubling: the tracking exercise does indeed reveal that recent waves are not acquiring valuable skills at the same rate as earlier waves did. If correct, this conclusion would have long-term implications for the economic and social impacts of immigration.

The available evidence indicates that whatever is going on in the low-skill labor market can only partially account for the slowdown. In particular, it is possible to calculate the wage growth of immigrants and natives after adjusting the data for the deteriorating conditions that low-skill workers face.[12] As Table 5.1 shows, there is still a substantial drop in the rate at which immigrant earnings are catching up, even after labor market conditions are taken into account. The wage growth of the typical immigrant who arrived in the late 1970s is twice as large as that of the late-1990s arrival.

Part of the slowdown, therefore, reflects a decline in how fast immi-

TABLE 5.1. WAGE IMPROVEMENT IN FIRST
TEN YEARS (RELATIVE TO NATIVES)

Immigrant wave	Increase in wages (percent)	
	Not accounting for changing economic conditions	Accounting for changing economic conditions
1975–79 arrivals	11.7	9.0
1995–99 arrivals	2.5	4.0

Source: George J. Borjas, "The Slowdown in the Economic Assimilation of Immigrants: Aging and Cohort Effects Revisited Again," *Journal of Human Capital* 9 (2015): 491.

grants are acquiring marketable new skills and qualifications. In fact, the rate at which immigrants become fluent in English has *also* slowed down. At the time of entry, about 30 percent of each immigrant wave in the past few decades spoke English fluently. Despite the similarity in entry conditions, the newer waves are not picking up English fluency as fast as the earlier waves did (see Figure 5.2). For the immigrants who came in the late 1970s, the fraction who spoke English fluently increased by 12 percentage points during their first decade in the country. For those who arrived in the late 1990s, the fraction increased by only 3 percentage points over an equivalent period of time.

The account of an undocumented Mexican immigrant who migrated to Iowa as a teenager elucidates how conditions on the ground can change the incentives to assimilate quickly:

I think there was just one Hispanic family in our high school besides mine. It was difficult to learn English, but it was easier compared to some people today. I had no translators, and the other Hispanic students in high school wouldn't talk to me in Spanish. We pretty much had to speak English right away. We had to figure it out on

FIGURE 5.2. ASSIMILATION AND ENGLISH FLUENCY

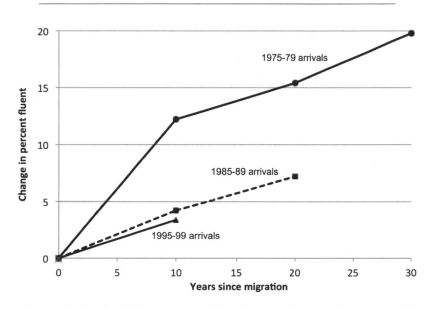

Source: Author's calculations using the 1980–2000 decennial censuses and the pooled 2009–2011 American Community Surveys.

our own, so we picked up more that way. . . . Now a lot of people don't even have to speak English. . . . Some of them don't even make an effort.[13]

It is tempting to dismiss the modern evidence of the assimilation slowdown by going back to the historical record and asserting that the immigrants who entered the country at the turn of the twentieth century experienced remarkable assimilation, and asking why the present should be any different. It is indeed widely believed that the economic performance of those immigrants improved dramatically during their lifetime, with some claiming that the entry wage gap between the Ellis Island–era immigrants and natives vanished within fifteen years.[14]

A recent reexamination of the data, however, shows that this widespread perception is wrong. The public release of the census manuscripts compiled at the time enables modern historians to track specific *persons* from census to census. For example, a man by the name of James Alexander who migrated from Wales in 1894 can be found in the 1900, 1910, and 1920 census manuscripts, and each of those censuses reports the kind of job that Mr. Alexander held. This person-level tracking lets us inspect the career path of each immigrant and compare it to the native path.

The tracking exercise turns the widespread perception of rapid assimilation on its head. As economic historians Ran Abramitzky, Leah Platt Boustan, and Katharine Eriksson conclude:

> The notion that European immigrants converged with natives after spending 10 to 15 years in the US is . . . exaggerated, as we find that initial immigrant-native occupational gaps persisted over time. . . . This pattern casts doubt on the conventional view that, in the past, immigrants who arrived with few skills were able to invest in themselves and succeed in the US economy within a single generation.[15]

In short, the historical experience provides surprisingly little evidence of *any* economic improvement for the Ellis Island immigrants during their lifetime.

The century-long perspective on assimilation trends sends a very intriguing message. It seems that only the immigrants who entered the United States *in between* the two mass migrations that serve as bookends to the twentieth century experienced substantial economic improvement during their lifetime. Those years happen to coincide with a period when, for a number of reasons, there was a lull in immigration. This observation raises a question with important implications: *Why?*

3. ASSIMILATION AND EDUCATION

BEFORE SPECULATING ON potential answers, let me first point out an obvious fact: average trends in economic assimilation mask vast differences across immigrant groups. Just as the entry wage differs dramatically between the typical Mexican and Russian immigrant, so does the assimilation rate.

It is easy to document this variation by tracking specific groups between 2000 and 2010. Consider, for example, the group of men born in Korea who were about thirty years old when they arrived in the United States in the late 1990s.* We can use the 2000 census to measure their economic performance at the time of entry. We can then observe those men again in the 2010 census, when they were about forty years old and had been in the country for ten years. Comparing their performance to that of comparably aged natives tells us how much catching up took place. We can then replicate the calculation for other immigrant groups to see how the catch-up rate differed across groups.

Figure 5.3 shows the link between economic assimilation and education. Note the huge variation in assimilation rates across the groups. The relative wage of Chinese immigrants grew by almost 30 percentage points in the first decade. By contrast, the growth rate was −6 percent for Cubans, −10 percent for Mexicans, and +17 percent for Indians.

Why do some groups assimilate quickly, while other groups lag behind? Skills obviously matter. Highly educated immigrants probably find it easier to acquire additional skills, such as becoming fluent in English or learning about available labor market opportunities. In other words, there is a complementarity between the skills that an immigrant has already acquired and the skills that he or she will acquire in the future.

---

* The tracking exercise shown in Figures 5.3 and 5.4 uses the sample of immigrant men who arrived between 1995 and 1999 and were twenty-five to thirty-four years old at the time of the 2000 census. The immigrants are compared to native men aged twenty-five to thirty-four in 2000.

FIGURE 5.3. WAGE GROWTH AND EDUCATION

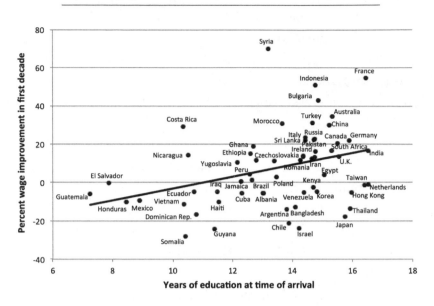

Source: Author's calculations using the 2000 decennial census and the pooled 2009–2011 American Community Surveys.

4. ASSIMILATION AND THE ETHNIC ENCLAVE

THE PAYOFF FOR acquiring new skills depends on how often the immigrants expect to use those new talents in their everyday interactions. Edward Lazear formalized this argument:

> Common culture and common language facilitate trade between individuals. Individuals have incentives to learn the other languages and cultures so that they have a larger pool of potential trading partners. The value of assimilation is larger to an individual from a small minority than to one from a large minority group. . . . Assimilation is less likely when an immigrant's native culture and language are broadly represented in his or her new country.[16]

Beneath the economic jargon, the idea is obvious. Immigrants who arrive in the United States and find few ethnic compatriots have a stronger incentive to acquire the tools necessary for a broader range of social and economic interactions, such as becoming fluent in English. In contrast, immigrants who find a large and welcoming ethnic enclave have much less need to acquire those tools; they already have a built-in audience that values whatever it is they brought with them.

The potential size of the ethnic enclave obviously depends not only on the total number of immigrants from a particular country, but also on how those immigrants are geographically scattered. In other words, it matters if the 1 million Cuban immigrants all settled in the same city, or if they are randomly dispersed across 300 cities. If there is extreme geographic clustering, even numerically small immigrant groups can offer a vibrant ethnic community to a newcomer.

One simple way of predicting the size of the ethnic enclave that a new arrival will live in is to look at the settlement pattern of the earlier immigrant waves: How many compatriots would a new immigrant find if he or she settled in the same metropolitan area as the average member of that group? As Figure 5.4 shows, immigrants who are welcomed by many ethnic compatriots take longer to become fluent in English.

It seems self-evident that a new immigrant has fewer incentives to acquire skills that are valuable outside the enclave if he or she can already interact with a large number of ethnic compatriots. Nevertheless, some observers insist that the ethnic enclave could still be economically beneficial. This perspective is associated with the work of Alejandro Portes, a prominent sociologist at Princeton University:

> Once an enclave has fully developed, it is possible for a newcomer to live his entire life within the confines of the community. Work, education, and access to health care, recreation, and a variety of other services can be found without leaving the boundaries of the ethnic economy. This institutional completeness is what enables new immigrants to move ahead economically.[17]

FIGURE 5.4. ENGLISH FLUENCY AND ETHNIC ENCLAVES

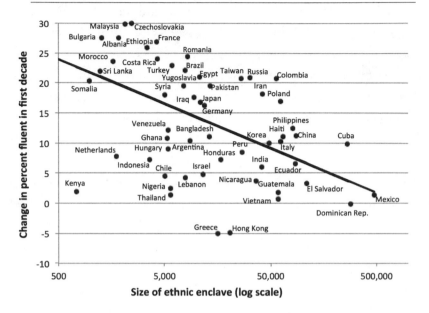

Source: Author's calculations using the 2000 decennial census and the
pooled 2009–2011 American Community Surveys.

In a sense, the "institutional completeness" of the enclave lets it
function separately from the rest of the economy, and immigrants
do not lose all that much by focusing their efforts within the ethnic
community. Given my personal experience with ethnic enclaves, I
am very sympathetic to this line of thinking. An enclave does indeed
meet many of the immigrant's needs during a difficult transition,
ranging from medical services to social contacts to simply looking
out for one another. All of these services can be very valuable to the
immigrant.

These benefits of the enclave, however, are often not captured by
the very narrow yardstick of wage growth. In terms of pure economic
achievement, the data do not cooperate with the prediction that the
enclave enables immigrants to "move ahead economically." Instead,
the evidence suggests that wages grow least for the immigrants who
live in large ethnic enclaves, making the enclave something of an eco-

nomic trap. Put bluntly, the geographic clustering of immigrant groups slows down their assimilation, and immigrants could get better-paying jobs by offering their services to a wider array of employers. In the words of a well-cited study: "Immigrant-minority workers in the open economy tend to receive higher returns to human capital than immigrant-minority workers in an ethnic enclave economy."[18]

This link between assimilation and the ethnic enclave has been used to explain the different experiences of immigrants in New York City and other metropolitan areas:

> What makes New York City so adept at integrating immigrants into the mainstream? . . . The city's immigrants come from every corner of the globe, and no single group makes up more than 12% of the foreign-born population. That makes it tough for any . . . group to form an isolated enclave. . . . It's a different story in the nation's "new" immigrant destinations. In places like Atlanta, the shared experiences . . . don't happen all that often.[19]

The *Harvard Encyclopedia of American Ethnic Groups* makes the same point in the context of Italian immigration in the early 1900s: "Newcomers from each locality tried to settle in the same street or tenement and to get jobs in the same factory but did not always succeed. They learned to meet and mingle with other Italians as well as with the Irish, Germans, Poles, and Scandinavians who lived and worked nearby . . . few neighborhoods were inhabited exclusively by Italians."[20]

I began this chapter by citing Samuel Huntington's controversial speculations about the assimilation prospects of Mexican immigrants. Huntington sparked a debate that continues to this day. In 2015, for example, the *Economist* revived the discussion by pointing out that Huntington had "published a bleak and at times nasty book about Mexican immigrants to America, fretting about their numbers, their Catholic values, their fertility and the threat they posed to the English language."[21]

The evidence summarized here could be interpreted as indicating that some concern is warranted. After all, Mexicans do have slower rates of wage growth and of becoming fluent in English than do many other groups. At the same time, however, the trend lines in the graphs that link assimilation to skills or to the size of the enclave (Figures 5.3 and 5.4) do not indicate that Mexicans are an "outlier" group; their experience is pretty much what the trend lines would predict.

In other words, Mexicans are assimilating and picking up the English language at the rate one would expect, *given the conditions they face when making assimilation decisions.* The fact that Mexican immigrants are disproportionately low-skill suggests that it will take longer for them to catch up. The very large Mexican enclaves will also slow down assimilation. But the slower catch-up rate has nothing to do with their being Mexican, and everything to do with the skills they brought and the social environment they face.

It would be unwise to dismiss Huntington's warning that the economic progress of Mexican immigrants may be lagging. But at the same time, it would be wrong to link those outcomes to the "Mexican-ness" of the flow. One often hears arguments that Mexicans are "special" because they are only a day's drive away from home or have deep-rooted historical links to parts of the southwestern United States. But the data do not support this notion. Mexicans are making the same assimilation decisions that other immigrant groups would make if they faced the same underlying circumstances.

Given the link between the ethnic enclave and economic assimilation, it would not be surprising if the persistence of large-scale immigration was partly responsible for the assimilation slowdown. The rapid growth in the size of many ethnic enclaves has reduced the incentives of new immigrants to obtain the talents that would be valued in the broader economy. A detailed analysis of the data, however, suggests that the growth of enclaves can account for less than a third of the slowdown.[22] Put bluntly, we do not yet fully understand why the slowdown occurred.

Before concluding this discussion, it is worth noting that the evidence reported in this chapter seems to contradict the widespread perception, fueled by the prevailing narrative, that immigrant assimilation is rapid, and that there is as much assimilation going on today as there used to be. For example, in the fall of 2015, the National Academy of Sciences published a report on immigrant assimilation that led the editorial board of the *Wall Street Journal* to gloat:

> Sorry to break the good news to some of our conservative friends, but it turns out that most immigrants to America are assimilating as their forebears did. That's the gist of a new 400-page report from the National Academies of Sciences, Engineering and Medicine. . . . Here's the money sentence: "Across all measurable outcomes, integration increases over time, with immigrants becoming more like the native-born with more time in the country."[23]

Similarly, the *New York Times,* in an article headlined "Newest Immigrants Assimilating as Fast as Previous Ones," summarized the evidence like this: "Immigrants' education levels, the diversity of their jobs, their wages and their mastery of English improved as they lived for more time in the United States."[24]

Of course, one needs to look specifically at the fine print of what the NAS report actually said to determine whether these interpretations tell the whole story. Here are some other "money sentences" from the NAS report itself that characterize *its* take on the evidence:

> Immigrants do experience earnings growth as length of residency increases, but they do not fully catch up to the native-born.

> Spanish-speakers and their descendants appear to be integrating more slowly in terms of both gaining English language and losing the ability to speak the immigrant language than other immigrant groups. . . . A major reason is the larger size and frequent replenishment of the Spanish-speaking population in the United States. . . .

Spanish speakers appear to become English proficient at a slower pace than other immigrants.[25]

In other words, economic assimilation does not fully overcome the sometimes very large entry disadvantage. And some immigrant groups, particularly groups welcomed by very large ethnic enclaves, are less inclined to acquire the valuable skills that would hasten the assimilation process. There is, in fact, little disagreement in the findings. It all depends on the spin.

5. A HISTORICAL SPECULATION

THE HISTORICAL RECORD suggests that neither the immigrants who entered the country as part of the mass migration before 1920 nor those who entered as part of the mass migration after 1980 experienced rapid rates of economic improvement after arrival. This century-long perspective indicates that substantial improvement *during an immigrant's working life* is atypical and can be found only among immigrants who entered the country in the interregnum between the two mass migrations.

We do not yet know which factors are most responsible for this remarkable pattern. But the evidence suggests some thoughts about assimilation that are worth pondering.

First, rapid economic improvement during an immigrant's lifetime is not a universal aspect of the immigrant experience, even in a country like the United States, which is typically thought of as being very socially and economically mobile.

Second, immigrants assimilate when the incentives to do so are particularly strong, and they do not when there is less need for assimilation (as when there are large ethnic enclaves).

Third, it is tempting to conjecture that the presence of mass migration before 1920 and after 1980 hindered the economic progress of those immigrant waves. Notably, the interval between those two migrations happens to be the period when restrictive immigration policies, combined with the economic debacle of the Great Depression and the political upheaval of World War II, greatly limited the number of immigrants.

A fascinating question remains open for future debate: Could it be that the limited immigration during that hiatus was partly responsible for the economic flourishing experienced by the immigrants who came in those years?

6

The Melting Pot

T HE IMAGE OF the United States as a melting pot dates as far back as the nation itself. In his classic *Letters from an American Farmer*, published in 1782, French immigrant Michel Guillaume Jean de Crèvecoeur wrote:

> What then is the American, this new man? . . . I could point out to you a family whose grandfather was an Englishman, whose wife was Dutch, whose son married a French woman, and whose present four sons have four wives of different nations. *He* is an American. . . . Here individuals are melted into a new race of men, whose labours and posterity will one day cause great change in the world.[1]

It is difficult to overstate the hold that this image—the melting of differences and the forging of a new man—has had on the American psyche. Given this mythic perspective, it seems almost inevitable that Israel Zangwill's popular play *The Melting Pot* opened in New York in 1908 at the peak of the Ellis Island era. The play greatly popularized the metaphor: Russian immigrants David and Vera fall in love. David is Jewish, and Vera is Christian. Vera's father, however, was involved in the pogrom that pushed David out of Russia. But in America love conquers all. David and Vera are reconciled and jointly proclaim the spiritual power of the melting pot as the sun sets over the Statue of Liberty.

Despite David and Vera's fairy-tale reconciliation, the ethnic diversity of that mass migration also provoked fears that the melting pot would no longer work. It did not take long for those fears to devolve into racist commentaries on the perceived inferiority of the new immigrants. In *The Passing of the Great Race*, the 1916 book that is perhaps the most influential statement of those anxieties, Madison Grant wrote:

> These new immigrants were no longer exclusively members of the Nordic race as were the earlier ones who came of their own impulse to improve their social conditions. The transportation lines advertised America as a land flowing with milk and honey and the European governments took the opportunity to unload upon careless, wealthy, and hospitable America the sweepings of their jails and asylums. The result was that the new immigration . . . contained a large and increasing number of the weak, the broken and the mentally crippled of all races drawn from the lowest stratum of the Mediterranean basin and the Balkans, together with hordes of the wretched, submerged populations of the Polish ghettos.[2]

Those fears led to the enactment of severe immigration restrictions by the early 1920s, leading Grant to proudly boast in the fourth edition of the book that "one of the most far-reaching effects" of his work was the adoption of "discriminatory and restrictive measures against the immigration of undesirable races and peoples."[3]

Fast-forward a century, and there is no longer any concern about the integration or economic performance of the descendants of the immigrants from the "wretched Polish ghettos." Somehow, many of the differences that differentiated those groups withered away. Nevertheless, the resurgence of mass migration in the past few decades has rekindled the debate. Demographers project that the children of current immigrants will make up at least 18 percent of the population by the year 2065.[4]

One side of the modern debate takes a long-term perspective and notes that although our ancestors shared those concerns, somehow things worked out. For example, the *Wall Street Journal*'s editorial board argues:

> Fears that the newest arrivals are overrunning America and changing it for the worse have a long pedigree. . . . It's true that many on the left promote a separate Hispanic identity, but their impact is small compared to the great assimilating maelstrom of American culture and economic life.[5]

Others seem less confident. Writing in the *Washington Post*, Robert Samuelson observed: "One of America's glories is that it has assimilated many waves of immigrants. . . . But I am not a foolish optimist. Assimilation requires time and the right conditions. It cannot succeed if we constantly flood the country with new, poor immigrants."[6] And in a blog entry at the libertarian Cafe Hayek on May 23, 2006, economist Russ Roberts blames the role that some government policies increasingly play in the immigrant's assimilation decision: "Legislation of various kinds has made it easier to stay unassimilated and encourages people to identify either culturally or politically with their own ethnic groups."[7]

Obviously, the concerns over the long-term workings of the melting pot are not purely economic. Nevertheless, the economic progress of immigrant families across generations is easy to measure, receives a great deal of attention, and is probably related to assimilation in other dimensions. In order to experience economic progress, the immigrant family will need to make choices, such as whether to adopt the English language, perhaps move away from ethnic enclaves, and espouse the cultural norms of American life.

Those choices, however, are not made in a vacuum. They occur in an environment that is specific to time and place. It would be foolish indeed to presume that the cultural, political, and economic conditions that might have led to an efficient operation of the melting pot in twentieth-century America can be reproduced in other times and in other places. In an important sense, the historical experience provides remarkably little information about what we can expect to happen to the descendants of the immigrants from today's mass migration.

1. HOW DO THE CHILDREN DO?

IT IS WIDELY believed that the economic status of the children of immigrants far surpasses that of their parents. After all, those children are typically the first in their families to be natively fluent in the English language, to acquire their education in American schools, and to instinctively learn at an early age what it takes to be successful in the US labor market.

The perception of substantial improvement between immigrants and their children is often based on a comparison of the two groups *at a point in time*. For example, the available census-type data in 2000 identifies two generations of Americans: the first generation composed of the immigrants themselves, and the second generation composed of persons born in the United States but who have at least one foreign-born parent. It is then straightforward to determine how workers in each generation are doing relative to the average worker in the labor market.

This type of calculation often leads to a very interesting finding. In the 2000 snapshot, for example, the typical immigrant earned 21 percent less than the average worker, while the typical second-generation worker earned 9 percent more. Put differently, the second generation earned about 30 percent more than the immigrant generation.

The superb performance of the second generation seems to imply—and is often interpreted as implying—that the children of immigrants do far better than their parents. The explanation goes along these lines: the immigrant experience has made those children "hungry," and they have the skills that ensure success in the US labor market.

There are indeed countless stories of the children of immigrants succeeding beyond all expectations. The stories often reference the key role that the immigrant experience played in their success. A recent news report in the *Daily Mail* contains inspiring sketches of the children of immigrants who were accepted to *all* Ivy League colleges in 2015.[7] One of these exceptional students, the child of former Target clerks who migrated from Nigeria, notes: "It was such a huge thing for my parents to uproot our family. . . . No matter how many times they got knocked down, they stayed positive, and kept telling me that the secret to success is unbridled resolve." An eighteen-year-old student whose parents migrated from Somalia explains: "The thing is, when you come here as an immigrant, you're hoping to have opportunities not only for yourself, but for your kids. . . . And that's always been at the back of my mind." Finally, a young man from Bulgaria echoes the sentiment: "My parents had done so much to put me in this position, to put me in the United States of America. . . . And I had to take advantage of that. I had to do something with the opportunities they gave me."

The 30 percent wage gap between the first and second generations is not driven solely by these exceptional and moving cases. Nevertheless, if that statistic were correct, it would suggest that concerns over the poor performance of recent immigrants might be misplaced. Their children could outperform the rest of the workforce in just a few decades.

Unfortunately, that 30 percent wage advantage does not justify this inference. As the discussion in the previous chapter showed, point-in-time comparisons of different groups of immigrants can provide very misleading information about what happens to a particular group over time. Given that my initial entry into immigration research was motivated by this conceptual problem, it did not take long for me to apply the same idea to a comparison of different generations.[8]

The main reason that the point-in-time comparison may be incorrect is obvious: the family ties between the first and second generations identifiable in a census snapshot are *very* tenuous. The typical second-generation worker in the 2000 snapshot was forty-two years old. But about 90 percent of the working immigrants enumerated in 2000 had arrived after 1970, making it *impossible* for them to have US-born children in their thirties or older. In other words, the average immigrant in 2000 cannot possibly be the parent of a working second-generation person enumerated at that same time, so there is no familial connection.

Ideally, we would like to link *specific* parents and children. The publicly available census data, however, do not permit this perfect linkage. Instead, researchers use statistical approximations that mimic a tracking of the immigrant population and its descendants across the decades.

As an example, the 1970 census reports how immigrants were doing at that time. Most of those immigrants arrived between 1940 and 1970 and could potentially be the parents of the second-generation workers found in the 2000 census. The comparison of the economic performance of immigrant workers in 1970 with the performance of second-generation workers a few decades later would then approximate the progress experienced by the children of *that* immigrant population.

As Table 6.1 shows, this tracking exercise indicates that the children of immigrants experienced a far more modest economic improve-

---

TABLE 6.1. TRACKING IMMIGRANTS ACROSS GENERATIONS

Year	Wage advantage of first generation (percent)	Wage advantage of second generation thirty years later (percent)
1940	+8.2	+17.1
1970	+1.5	+9.0
2000	−20.8	?

Source: George J. Borjas, *Immigration Economics* (Cambridge, MA: Harvard University Press, 2014), 193.

ment. In 1970, the typical immigrant earned 1.5 percent more than the average worker. By 2000, the typical second-generation worker earned 9 percent more. In other words, the intergenerational improvement was about 8 percent—rather than the 30 percent implied by the point-in-time comparison.

Similarly, the 1940 census reports that immigrants had a wage advantage of 8 percent. By 1970, the working children of those immigrants had a 17 percent wage advantage. Again, the intergenerational improvement between 1940 and 1970 is about 9 percent.

Extrapolating into the future leads to a less optimistic forecast for the children of the current wave. In 2000, immigrants had a wage disadvantage of over 20 percent. If the future improvement follows the historical pattern, the children of current immigrants will have a 10 percent wage *disadvantage* in 2030. If this projection comes true, the declining fortunes of the second generation—a group that is bound to grow substantially in the next few decades—will certainly become a central concern in the debate.

2. THE PERSISTENCE OF ETHNIC DIFFERENCES

THE AVERAGE ECONOMIC progress between immigrants and their children masks huge differences across immigrant groups. We know that there is a lot of ethnic inequality in the first generation. Not surprisingly, some of that inequality persists into the second generation, so ethnicity still helps determine the outcomes of the children. In 2010, for example, second-generation workers from Canada earned about 30 percent more than second-generation workers from the Dominican Republic.

A well-functioning melting pot should lead not only to upward mobility in the second generation—as in that 9 percent average wage gain between immigrants and their children—but also narrow the differences that exist among ethnic groups. If ethnic inequality was "sticky" over time, one would wonder whether the melting pot was doing its job.

Research on the stickiness of ethnicity has a long history, but the issue is still not fully resolved. Many studies that examined the progress of the descendants from the Ellis Island–era immigrants concluded that the country fused a collection of dissimilar groups into the native population in a relatively short time, perhaps two generations.[9] This conclusion, however, encountered both ideological objections about whether such an outcome was desirable, and methodological questions about whether the melting pot was really that efficient.

On the philosophical side, there is disagreement on the presumption that the melting pot is "good." The goal perhaps should not be a melting of differences, but a society where cultural pluralism rules, ethnic differences are celebrated, and the groups live in harmony. As early as 1915, Horace M. Kallen outlined this multicultural utopia in *The Nation*:

> Its form is that of the Federal republic; its substance a democracy of nationalities, cooperating voluntarily and autonomously in the enterprise of self-realization through the perfection of men according to their kind. . . . The United States are in the process of becoming a federal state not merely as a union of geographical and administrative unities, but also as a cooperation of cultural diversities, as a federation or commonwealth of national cultures.[10]

In addition to the ideological attack, the 1963 publication of Nathan Glazer and Daniel Moynihan's *Beyond the Melting Pot* sparked a debate that continues to this day over the actual effectiveness of the melting pot by boldly declaring: "The point about the melting pot is that it did not happen. . . . the American ethos is nowhere better perceived than in the disinclination of the third and fourth generation of newcomers to blend into a standard, uniform national type."[11]

In recent years, the concept of assimilation has been redefined, debated, and stretched in countless sociological studies, and many now accept that there are multiple modes of assimilation and that no single mode can describe the experience of all immigrant groups. As an example of this discussion, just think of what assimilation would mean for immigrants in racially distinct groups. Will the children of the immigrants from Jamaica or Haiti eventually approach the socioeconomic norm of white America, or the norm of the African American population? And which of these two outcomes would be considered assimilation?

Rather than dwell on the minutiae of this never-ending debate, it is more useful to get a larger perspective on the issue. What does tracking the performance of a *specific* group across generations tell us about the effectiveness of the melting pot—at least in terms of economic progress? For example, the 1980 census tells us how much Canadian immigrants earned at that time, and the 2010 snapshot reports earnings for the children of those immigrants. We can then repeat this exercise for other ethnic groups and observe the pattern that summarizes the link between immigrants and their children.

Figure 6.1 shows that the groups that fared well in the first generation fared well in the second, while the groups that fared poorly in the first fared poorly in the second.* The figure also suggests that the wage gap between any two groups is often smaller among the children than among the immigrants. For example, there is about a 30 percent wage gap between Haitian and Filipino immigrants. But the gap between the children of those two groups narrowed to 20 percent. In fact, the trend line linking the two generations implies that about 60 percent of the wage gap between any two immigrant groups persists into the second generation.

The previous chapter began the discussion of assimilation by noting Samuel Huntington's concerns about the integration of Mexican immigrants. As we saw, the data indicated that the economic assimilation of Mexican immigrants *during their lifetime* was what we would expect to

---

* In Figures 6.1 and 6.2, the age-adjusted wage differences are calculated in a sample of working men aged twenty-five to sixty-four who are not enrolled in school. This information is reported for the largest immigrant groups.

FIGURE 6.1. ETHNICITY AND THE CHILDREN OF IMMIGRANTS

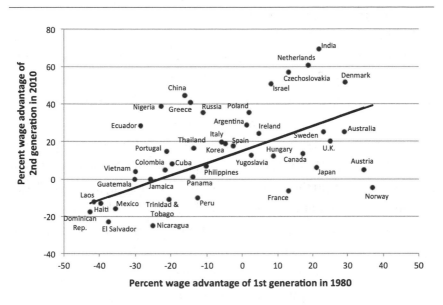

Source: Author's calculations using the 1980 decennial census and the pooled 2010–2013 March Current Population Surveys.

find for a group with that level of education and such large welcoming enclaves. The Mexican experience *across generations* is also not an outlier; the experience of the Mexican children is very close to the trend line. Those children are doing as well as could be expected, given the low starting point of the parents. In other words, there is nothing to suggest that the "Mexican-ness" of immigrants somehow affects the assimilation process—either within or across generations.

Although ethnic differences narrow, the melting pot's job is clearly not done after two generations. In fact, the historical experience of the immigrants who arrived at the turn of the twentieth century confirms that the ethnic inequality that characterized that mass migration persisted into the grandchildren's generation. The available data enable us to roughly track the descendants of the immigrants in the largest ethnic groups. The 1910 and 1920 censuses report the occupations of the immigrants, so it is easy to construct a measure of earning potential in the first generation. The General Social Surveys collected decades later (between 1972 and 2010) provide information on the grandchildren of those immigrants.

Figure 6.2 suggests that the groups that did well in 1920 had grandchildren who also did well eight decades later. There is much less ethnic inequality among the grandchildren than among the immigrants. A 30 percent wage gap existed between German and Mexican immigrants back in 1920. By 2000, the gap between the grandchildren of those groups had narrowed to 10 percent. In fact, the trend line indicates that only about a third of the wage gap between any two immigrant groups survived into the third generation. The melting pot worked, but it probably took about 100 years for all differences to disappear.

This long-term tracking exercise, however, faces one major challenge. The national origin of persons is clearly defined in the first generation; census data tell us *precisely* where each person was born. Even in the second generation, ethnic background is well defined; census

FIGURE 6.2. THE MELTING POT IN THE TWENTIETH CENTURY

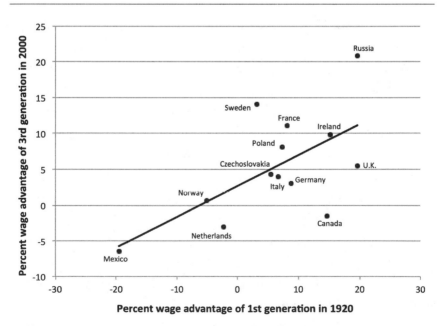

Source: Author's calculations using the pooled 1910–1920 decennial censuses and the pooled 1972–2010 General Social Surveys.

data tell us *precisely* where the parents were born. Once we move to the grandchildren of immigrants, however, the allocation of a grandchild to an ethnic group is no longer so clear-cut. The available surveys almost never ask: "Where were your grandparents born?" Instead, ethnicity typically comes from the answer to: "Where did your ancestors come from?" It is entirely possible that the identity we would select for someone based on the actual birthplace of his grandparents would differ from the ethnic label that the person chose to wear.

It has been documented that persons who have a well-defined Mexican ancestry and high levels of socioeconomic achievement tend to self-identify as Mexicans *less often* than do persons who have an equally well-defined Mexican ancestry but low levels of achievement. In a series of important studies, Brian Duncan and Stephen Trejo show that this *choice* in ethnic self-identification can badly contaminate measures of economic improvement across generations.[12]

In particular, the economic outcomes of those who call themselves "Mexicans" hides the true progress made by the group because some of the successful grandchildren decided to join a different group. Perhaps because of a higher incidence of intermarriage, many of those grandchildren classified themselves as non-Hispanic whites. And even though a few continued to call themselves Hispanics, they specifically failed to report any Mexican ancestry.

Had those descendants of Mexican immigrants remained "Mexican," we would probably find that the typical Mexican family experienced even more improvement than is indicated by the tracking exercise. Although the problem of ethnic "self-selection" is widely acknowledged to exist, we simply do not know how it has affected existing measures of long-term assimilation.

3. WHY IS ETHNICITY STICKY?

WE HAVE ALREADY seen that large ethnic enclaves reduce the incentives for immigrants to acquire skills that may be useful outside the enclave, slowing down assimilation during the immigrant's working life. But it is not only the size of the enclave that matters; its skill mix also plays a role. The ethnic neighborhood can form a type of social capital, called "ethnic capital," that influences the progress of future generations.[13]

It is easy to see how ethnic capital can play a role. Think of the situation facing the children of a hypothetical Mexican and a hypothetical Korean family. Both parents in these families are high school graduates, and they live in similarly sized Mexican and Korean neighborhoods. However, many of the residents in the Mexican enclave lack a high school education, while many of the residents in the Korean enclave have college diplomas.

It would not be surprising if the continued exposure to these different environments influenced the children's development. The children in this hypothetical example would then be on different paths. The Mexican child would be frequently exposed to the social and economic contacts that are common among low-educated workers, while the Korean child would be exposed to the contacts more common among college graduates. The ethnic environment acts like a magnet, "pulling" the child toward the average or norm in that particular ethnic group and increasing the stickiness in ethnic outcomes across generations. In fact, there is evidence that the average skills of an ethnic group *do* affect progress across generations, with membership in low-skill groups holding back children and membership in high-skill groups boosting them.

A natural experiment conducted in Sweden confirms that the skill composition of the enclave influences the economic outcomes of immigrant children. Between 1985 and 1994, Sweden randomly located new refugees across a large number of cities, rather than letting them settle in the traditional gateways, such as Stockholm and Malmö.[14] By chance, some refugees ended up in neighborhoods where their ethnic compatriots were a bit more skilled. It turns out that the children that were randomly assigned to neighborhoods where a higher fraction of the compatriots were better educated ended up doing far better in school.

Finally, a well-known sociological study tracked a number of Mexican families in the United States over four generations and documented another interesting way in which the ethnic environment helps preserve ethnic differences.[15] Living in a large ethnic enclave implies the presence of a large number of potential mates of the same ethnic background, reducing the likelihood of intermarriage.

The fact that ethnicity matters, and that the ethnic environment influences the economic progress of the immigrant family, raises problems for the immigrant-as-worker perspective. The notion of ethnicity is irrelevant if immigrants are just an army of raw labor inputs, filling labor needs wherever those needs arise. Outside the factory gate, however, there is a social, cultural, economic, and political entity called the ethnic enclave. Because immigrants cluster in those enclaves, and because the environment permeating those enclaves affects assimilation, the immigration of real-world human beings, who have ethnic roots and ethnic links, will inevitably have economic and cultural repercussions that can persist for many decades.

4. THE PAST AS A GUIDE TO THE FUTURE: SOME SPECULATIONS

SOME OBSERVERS LOOK at the history of the melting pot and fear that large chunks of the foreign-born population today may become a permanent underclass, experiencing poor economic and social outcomes generation after generation. Others look at the same history and conclude that the "assimilating maelstrom" of the melting pot will do its job.

Both of those inferences are probably wrong. The process of assimilation is partly the result of choices made by immigrant families, and those families choose the path that is most beneficial under a particular set of constraints, institutions, and circumstances.

The fact that assimilation is a choice forces us to acknowledge that the century-long integration of the Ellis Island–era immigrants happened under a unique set of circumstances. *And* it is far from clear that those unique circumstances can (or should) be reproduced. It is easy to illustrate the fragility of using the historical experience as a guide by pointing out some of those circumstances.

Most obvious, the immigrants who entered the country at the turn of the twentieth century faced dramatically different economic conditions than those entering today. Many of the immigrants who arrived in the early 1900s got jobs in the booming manufacturing sector. Those manufacturing jobs, which over time evolved into well-paid and stable union jobs, created a private-sector safety net that protected the pay and economic status of the immigrants and their children and grandchildren. In short, those manufacturing jobs were *the* gateway to the middle class for many immigrant families. One does not have to be a very perceptive observer to notice that the sectors employing low-skill immigrants today—particularly in a labor market that increasingly penalizes low-skill workers—do not offer the same type of protection that unionized manufacturing jobs provided back then.

Second, some of the large immigrant groups that arrived before the 1920s were "encouraged" to assimilate by the political upheaval related to the two world wars. The *Harvard Encyclopedia of American Ethnic Groups* notes: "By summer 1918 about half of the [US] states had restricted or eliminated German-language instruction, and several had curtailed freedom to speak German in public." Similarly, "the thirties were a time of conflict within Italian-American communities between the loyal supporters and the growing number of opponents to Mussolini's Fascism. The battle raged in the press, on the radio, in the meetings of Italian organizations, and occasionally in the streets."[16] It would be fascinating to find out whether these sudden shifts in social attitudes and tolerance toward specific groups had more than a negligible effect on assimilation, but there have been no careful examinations of the potential link.

Third, the explosive growth of the welfare state has probably altered the selection of persons choosing to migrate to the United States, as well as the selection of immigrants choosing to remain in the country. The changed incentives to migrate and to stay almost surely have changed the composition of the immigrant population. Moreover, the welfare state benefits many immigrants. Some of the social programs could boost immigrant economic performance by offering access to early-childhood education, better nutrition, and improved medical care. Unfortunately, the net association between the welfare state and long-term assimilation also has not been explored.

Finally, the ideological climate that presumably boosted assimilation throughout much of the twentieth century has disappeared. The consensus behind *E Pluribus Unum* ("out of many, one") is dead and gone.

A recent University of California (UC) directive to that institution's faculty and staff shows just how far we have traveled.[17] This document advised UC employees to avoid using phrases that can lead to "microaggressions" toward students and each other, where a microaggression is defined as "the everyday verbal, nonverbal, and environmental slights, snubs, or insults, whether intentional or unintentional, that communicate hostile, derogatory, or negative messages to target persons based solely upon their marginalized group membership."

A specific example given of a microaggression is the statement "America is a melting pot." Such a statement, the UC memo claims, sends a message to its recipients that they have to "assimilate to the dominant culture." It will be very interesting to see how such a radical ideological shift about the melting pot affects the integration of the new immigrants.

Despite what many might claim, absent a crystal ball it is impossible to do much more than speculate about the long-term prospects for today's immigrants. What I think we can conclude, however, is that the historical experience probably has little to teach us about the next few decades, and it should not be relied on to predict either a rosy future or a looming debacle. Instead, the lesson to keep in mind is that the melting pot will operate most efficiently when *that* outcome is in the immigrants' self-interest.

7

The Labor Market Impact

IMMIGRANTS DO JOBS that natives don't want to do. The libertarian Cato Institute says so: "Lower-skilled immigrants seek low-paying, low-status jobs that an insufficient number of Americans aspire to fill." The progressive Center for American Progress elaborates: "Immigrants and native-born workers don't compete against each other because they have different skill sets and ultimately hold different jobs." And even labor unions agree. The American Federation of State, County, and Municipal Employees asserts: "Immigrants do jobs that are not necessarily jobs that laid-off American workers would take." In fact, the American reluctance to do certain jobs is so intense that the state of California imports foreign-born temporary workers to design the system that processes the unemployment claims of those laid-off Americans.[1]

The science is settled. Immigrants do jobs that natives will not do and have little impact on native job opportunities as a result. Anyone who follows the immigration debate surely noticed this refrain getting louder in the past decade, as the political class considered various proposals that would grant amnesty to undocumented workers and substantially increase the number of visas in many categories. But there are some inconvenient facts that tend to be overlooked.

As part of an enforcement initiative by the Bush administration in September 2006, immigration agents raided a chicken-processing plant in Stillmore, Georgia. Like many other rural communities, Stillmore had attracted an increasing number of immigrants, including many who were undocumented. The *Wall Street Journal* sent a team of reporters a few months after the raid to investigate what had happened in the interim. The team gathered evidence that speaks volumes about how labor markets respond to supply shocks:

> After a wave of raids by federal immigration agents on Labor Day weekend, a local chicken-processing company called Crider Inc. lost 75% of its mostly Hispanic 900-member work force. The crackdown threatened to cripple the economic anchor of this fading rural town. But for local African-Americans, the dramatic appearance of federal agents presented an unexpected opportunity. Crider suddenly raised pay at the plant. An advertisement in the weekly *Forest-Blade* newspaper blared "Increased Wages" at Crider, starting at $7 to $9 an hour—more than a dollar above what the company had paid many immigrant workers.[2]

The ad, shown in Figure 7.1, demonstrates the common sense underlying the laws of supply and demand far better than the elaborate mathematical models of economists ever could. As the eighteenth-century English writer Samuel Johnson famously noted: "When a man knows he is to be hanged in a fortnight, it concentrates his mind wonderfully."[3] Faced with the possibility of being unable to operate the plant and suffering substantial losses, Crider did what any profit-maximizing firm would do: it tried to attract more workers by offering a higher wage.

Many of the replacement workers that Crider hired were African Americans. From Crider's perspective, the changed demographics were not all to the good:

> In the months since Crider began hiring hundreds of African-Americans . . . the plant has struggled with high turnover among

FIGURE 7.1. A FIRM'S RESPONSE
TO A CUT IN LABOR SUPPLY

Source: *Forest-Blade*, Swainsboro, GA; September 2006.

black workers, lower productivity and pay disputes between the new employees and labor contractors. The allure of compliant Latino workers willing to accept grueling conditions despite rock-bottom pay has proved a difficult habit for Crider to shake, particularly because the local, native-born workers who replaced them are more likely to complain about working conditions and aggressively assert what they believe to be legal pay and workplace rights.[4]

So what is the lesson that eludes the Cato Institute and the Center for American Progress but that Crider quickly grasped when it had to? It is not that immigrants do jobs that natives don't want to do. It is instead that immigrants do jobs that natives don't want to do *at the going wage.*

It is not difficult to come up with other inconvenient examples. Anyone who has ridden in a cab in New York City, where a third of the population is foreign-born, could easily infer that few natives want to drive cabs anymore. In 1970, 88 percent of all cab drivers in New York were natives; by 2010, 84 percent were immigrants. Cab driving, it seemed, had become a job that natives didn't want to do. As in Stillmore, this change affected many African Americans. Almost 20 percent of New York cabbies in 1970 were black; by 2010, only 6 percent were.

But do natives really refuse to drive cabs these days? What happened in cities that were less affected by immigration? In Philadelphia, just 100 miles south, only 10 percent of the population is foreign-born, and natives still make up 73 percent of all cabbies, with black natives accounting for a third. It may be cheaper to take a cab in New York, but the fact remains: natives *do* drive cabs.

We all have a threshold price that determines our willingness to do particular things in life. And it could be that those undocumented "compliant Latino workers" in Stillmore had a much lower threshold: they were willing to do more for less.

But it is also the case that markets react both to the presence of immigrants and to their absence. And this reaction may be the one that common sense suggests and that Crider pursued: firms will pay less when there is excess labor, and more when they need to attract workers.

So, what is the labor market impact of immigration? And are the commonsense implications of the laws of supply and demand actually observed in real-world labor markets?

Hundreds of published studies examine these questions. Some claim that immigration has little impact on native wages, while others argue that the effect is sizable. It is very instructive to expose the nature of the disagreements by showing what researchers actually do to get an answer. Much of what we think we know about the labor market impact is driven by assumptions. In some cases, amazing as it may seem, *the numerical answer has been assumed*, regardless of what the data actually say. The most credible evidence—based solely on the data—suggests that a 10 percent increase in the size of a skill group probably reduces the wage of that group by at least 3 percent.

1. THE HELICOPTER PARABLE

LET ME START with a parable that shows how economists think about the labor market impact of immigration. The parable has the added benefit that it suggests how we can measure the impact in real-world labor markets. Furthermore, it clarifies what the conditions on the ground must have been if we are to believe those estimates.

A *very big* helicopter flies around the United States after we settle in for a night's sleep. This helicopter is superfast, flying vast distances in nanoseconds. And it is on a haphazard journey: Sometimes it turns right, sometimes left. Sometimes it stops and hovers, more or less randomly. When the helicopter comes to a stop in midair, its side doors open and a random number of persons—sometimes a small number, sometimes a large number—parachute off into the night. Those jumpers are immigrants making their way to their new homes. By sunrise, the helicopter has done its job: its human cargo has been delivered to random places in random quantities across this large country, and the helicopter disappears from sight.

We are the natives. We wake up in the morning and notice that our town has changed. Before we went to bed the night before, our city had about 1 million workers. Now our city has 1.1 million of them—a supply shock of 10 percent. What happens when we and the firms that employ us discover that there are a lot more people looking for work than there were the day before?

Let's first think of what might happen that morning *immediately* after we wake up, before anyone has time to react. This snapshot obviously does not capture the whole story. Native workers, for example, might eventually react by moving to (or away from) cities that the helicopter bypassed, or by trying to acquire credentials that will differentiate them from the immigrants. Employers might expand the size of the office or factory to take advantage of the new workers. For now, however, let's put all those reactions aside and focus on the short run, the period of time that immediately follows the helicopter drop.

In this short run, much will depend on who the immigrants are and how they compare to native workers like us. The town we live in is one of those homogeneous towns where everybody produces widgets. We produce widgets, our neighbors produce widgets, and all the factories are widget-producing factories. And now there are 100,000 new workers. Do they make widgets too? Are the immigrants clones of our productive selves?

Suppose that the two groups are indeed clones of each other—or, as an economist would put it, immigrants and natives are "perfect substitutes."* What does common sense then tell us?

There are now a lot more widget-making workers in this widget-producing town. When everyone shows up for work, employers notice a lot more people trying to fill the slots on the assembly line. In the short run, employers squeeze new workers into the existing infrastructure so that more widgets can be produced. After all, the immigrants are consumers too and will buy some of those extra widgets. But the employers, who are always looking to make a buck, also find that they can get away with paying a lower wage because many more workers are available. In the short run, immigration reduces the wage of native workers who are productive clones of the immigrants.

This conclusion, of course, is just a restatement of the laws of supply and demand. If the supply of oil goes up, the price of gas goes down. If the supply of workers goes up, the price of workers—the wage that employers pay—also goes down. Few dispute the obvious link between the supply of oil and the price of gas. But because of its political implications, the restatement of the same idea in the immigration context is widely contested.

---

* The technical definition of "perfect substitutes" is subtler than is implied by the productive-clones analogy. Two groups are perfect substitutes as long as one can be exchanged for the other at a constant (and not necessarily one-to-one) rate.

This parable contains many assumptions that lead to the predicted decline in native wages. A crucial one is that natives and immigrants are clones. This need not be the case. Perhaps the immigrants have skills that are unsuited for producing widgets, but perfectly suited for mowing our lawns or helping us raise our children. What will happen then?

Before the helicopter drop, *we* mowed the lawn and *we* took care of the children. But now the immigrants can take on those tasks, freeing us to do what we do best—namely, produce widgets. Natives and immigrants, therefore, are "complements" in production. The helicopter drop gives us more time to think about how to make widgets better and faster, making us more productive and worth more to our employers.

When we show up at the factory, our employers notice that we are more refreshed and have even come up with ideas about how to improve production. They reward our increased productivity by bidding for our new and improved services, raising our wage in the process. In short, immigration increases the wage of native workers if immigrants and natives are complements.

Of course, in any real-world supply shock, some natives will be substitutes and others will be complements. A supply shock of low-skill immigrants, for instance, would probably substitute for the native low-skill workforce, but would likely complement native high-skill workers. According to the laws of supply and demand, then, in the short run the wage of low-skill natives would fall and the wage of high-skill natives would rise.

2. THE *MARIELITOS*

THE HELICOPTER PARABLE suggests that, to measure what immigration actually does to wages, we should look at what happens in different places. If natives and immigrants are substitutes, we should see the wage drop in cities that received many immigrants relative to what happens in cities that received few. But if the two groups are complements, we should see the wage rising in towns that received many immigrants.

This is, in fact, the approach used by many researchers. And the classic study in this genre is economist David Card's analysis of what happened to Miami after the Mariel boatlift.[5] In this case, it was not a helicopter that randomly hovered over Miami and dropped a large number of immigrants, but a flotilla run by Cuban Americans who desperately wanted to bring their relatives to the United States.

On April 20, 1980, Fidel Castro declared that Cubans wishing to move to the United States could leave from the port of Mariel. The first *Marielitos* arrived on April 23. By June 3, over 100,000 Cubans had migrated, and Miami's workforce had grown by about 8 percent. We can determine the impact of the flotilla "drop" by looking at labor market conditions in Miami just before and after the event.

Figure 7.2 illustrates the trend in the (inflation-adjusted) hourly wage of white workers in Miami. In 1979, just prior to Mariel, the typical worker earned about $6.40 per hour, and the same was true after Mariel in 1981. There was a slight decline, to $6.20 an hour, in 1982, and the wage remained constant at that level through 1985.

Of course, it is hard to interpret the trend in Miami's wages unless we compare it to what was going on elsewhere, during those early years of the Reagan administration. Put differently, we need to know what happened in a "control group," a set of cities unaffected by the flotilla drop. It is entirely possible, for example, that the wage was growing rapidly in other cities, and that Miami's workers missed out because of Mariel. The control group acts like the placebo in a medical experiment. For reasons that I will discuss shortly, Card picked Atlanta, Houston, Los Angeles, and Tampa–St. Petersburg to form the placebo.

The wage in the placebo cities rose slightly after 1982, but the relative position of Miami's workforce was not much worse for the wear. In 1979, the typical worker in Miami earned 50 cents less per hour than the typical worker in the placebo. By 1985, the gap was 60 cents, a trivial difference of 10 cents an hour, or $4 for a full workweek. Not surprisingly, Card concluded: "The distribution of non-Cubans' wages in the Miami labor market was remarkably stable between 1979 and

FIGURE 7.2. MARIEL AND THE
EARNINGS OF WHITE WORKERS

The placebo cities are Atlanta, Houston, Los Angeles,
and Tampa–St. Petersburg.

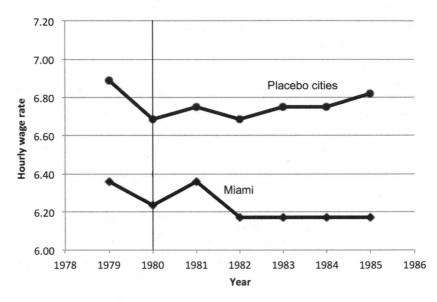

Source: Adapted from David Card, "The Impact of the Mariel Boatlift on the
Miami Labor Market," *Industrial and Labor Relations Review* 43 (1990): 250.

1985. . . . These data provide little evidence of a negative effect of the
Mariel influx on the earnings of natives."[6]

Because of its obvious intuition and simplicity, the Mariel study has
played a crucial role in building the narrative that immigration is "good
for everyone." As recently as 2014, President Obama's Council of Economic Advisers (CEA) prepared a report to justify the president's execu-
tive actions granting amnesty to millions of undocumented workers. The
Obama-appointed economists trumpeted that the Mariel study

examines the effect of a large influx of lower-skilled immigrants—
the arrival of 125,000 Cuban immigrants in the 1980 Mariel boatlift, which increased the labor force in Miami by 7 percent—on

the labor market opportunities of native workers nationwide. The author finds no effect on the likelihood of employment of lower-skilled, non-Cuban workers. . . . Average wages for natives rose by 0.6 percent on the whole following the Mariel boatlift.[7]

Although the Mariel study is the best known, many other researchers have compared outcomes between cities where few immigrants live and cities where many immigrants live. There is a huge disparity in what those studies report, but the evidence seems to cluster around a simple result: the wage falls in cities where the helicopter dropped many immigrants, but the effect is small.

The helicopter parable, however, suggests that it would be foolish to bet the farm on conclusions drawn from these nonexperimental studies. After all, the real-world helicopter is not on a haphazard journey, randomly dropping many people in San Diego and few in Philadelphia. The geographic sorting of immigrants is *not* random. Immigrants are more likely to settle in high-wage cities than in cities with stagnant labor markets. This locational choice builds in a spurious correlation—higher pay, more immigrants—that makes it harder to detect when immigration lowers the wage of competing workers.

Moreover, natives will respond to the supply shock. Native workers in San Diego, for example, may find that immigrants have reduced their wage, and many such workers will pack up and move to cities that the helicopter bypassed, taking some of the wage pressure off San Diego and moving it elsewhere. Similarly, employers might relocate to cities where immigration offers the potential for higher profits. All of these reactions, which inevitably occur as we move from the short run to the long run, help diffuse the impact of immigration throughout the US economy.

3. IMMIGRATION AND SKILLS

IN AN IMMIGRATION researcher's perfect world, random supply shocks such as Mariel would happen frequently. We could then exploit these natural experiments to measure the impact of immigration by comparing the affected localities with unaffected placebos. In real life, however, such events are rare, so we have devoted a lot of time and effort to figuring out other ways of measuring the impact. In fact, I spent much of the 1990s trying to crack this problem, often in collaboration with my Harvard colleagues Richard Freeman and Lawrence Katz.[8] By the end of the decade, I knew that a solution would require that we take into account the fact that immigrants and natives bring different capabilities to the labor market.

We can be certain of one thing about that morning after the helicopter drop: there are a lot more workers in the country. Some of them are highly educated, and some have little education. Some are young, and some are old.

It is very hard for natives to respond to an influx of workers by switching across skill groups. A twenty-year-old native cannot suddenly turn forty-five to escape competition from young immigrants. A low-educated native cannot acquire a college degree overnight. And a college graduate cannot magically turn into a doctor. Those barriers mean that natives are somewhat stuck in a particular skill group, and there is little leeway for them to react to the helicopter drop.

I started looking more carefully at immigration trends across education and age groups and noticed that the helicopter drop had increased the size of some groups substantially, but had barely changed the size of other groups. The helicopter parable now suggested a different way for measuring the impact: looking at wages in specific skill groups before and after the helicopter drop to see whether the wage changes have anything to do with who the immigrants were. Put simply, we want to explore whether the wage trends across education and age groups are related to immigration trends across those groups.

This is precisely the method I proposed in a study published in 2003.[9] The publication of that paper created a stir because it was the first to provide credible evidence that the laws of supply and demand apply in the immigration context.[10] In other words, wages grow least in the skill groups that receive the most immigrants.

Suppose we categorize workers into skill groups by education and age. On the education side, let's specify five groups: high school dropouts, high school graduates, some college education, college graduates, and some postcollege education. Age is also relevant because workers who are young are not clones of those who are old. In terms of age, let's classify workers into eight groups defined by the amount of work experience: 1–5 years, 6–10 years, 11–15 years, and so on. We can then assign each worker to one of 40 different skill groups (5 education groups multiplied by 8 age groups).

It is easy to see how the earnings growth of those skill groups is related to immigration. The decennial census data between 1960 and 2010 enable us to calculate the average change in annual earnings of native workers in each group from one census to the next. Figure 7.3 shows that earnings grew most for the skill groups least affected by immigration, and grew least for the groups most affected. The trend line suggests that if immigration increases the size of a group by 10 percent, the earnings of native workers in that group fall by 3–4 percent.

There is an obvious contradiction between the evidence from the Mariel natural experiment and the decades-long relation between wages and immigration illustrated in Figure 7.3. If immigration were to have an impact, the Miami of the early 1980s would seem the obvious place to find it. This paradox inspired me to revisit the Mariel episode while writing this book. To my shock, within an hour after I started looking at the publicly available data, my computer screen was flashing very strong evidence that the Mariel study, published a quarter century ago, was plain wrong. In fact, Mariel had substantially lowered the wage of low-skill workers in Miami.[11]

The key to unlocking the Mariel puzzle was the simple insight emphasized in my 2003 study: skills matter. Almost two-thirds of the *Marielitos* were high school dropouts, so the Mariel supply shock increased the number of high school dropouts in the Miami area by an astounding 18 percent in a matter of weeks. This observation suggested that looking at what happened to the wage of high school

FIGURE 7.3. EARNINGS OF NATIVE WORKERS
AND IMMIGRATION

The average annual earnings of a skill group are calculated
in a sample of native men aged eighteen to sixty-four who
are not enrolled in school. The immigrant share is the
percentage of workers who are foreign-born in a skill group.
The figure removes decade effects.

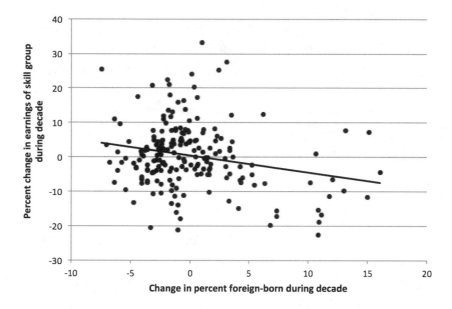

Source: Author's calculations using the 1960–2000 decennial censuses and the
pooled 2008–2012 American Community Surveys.

dropouts would be a good place to start. Remarkably, that trivial comparison had not been made in Card's original study or in any other
replication of that analysis.

As Figure 7.4 shows, the earnings of the workers most likely to be
affected by the *Marielitos* plummeted after 1980, and it took a decade
for that wage to fully recover. The wage drop was sizable. The (inflation-
adjusted) weekly wage of high school dropouts in Miami fell by about

FIGURE 7.4. MARIEL AND THE EARNINGS OF HIGH SCHOOL DROUPOUTS

Average weekly earnings are calculated in a sample of non-Hispanic men who lack a high school diploma and are twenty-five to fifty-nine years old. The cities in the Card placebo are Atlanta, Houston, Los Angeles, and Tampa–St. Petersburg. The cities in the employment placebo are Anaheim, Rochester (New York), Nassau-Suffolk, and San Jose. The data are smoothed using a three-year moving average.

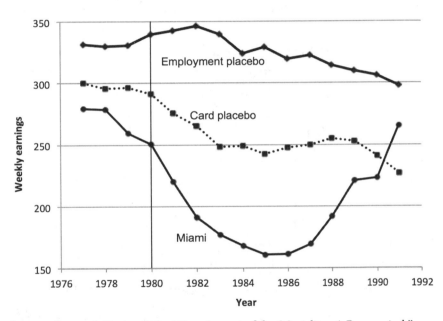

Source: George J. Borjas, "The Wage Impact of the *Marielitos*: A Reappraisal," National Bureau of Economic Research Working Paper no. 21588, September 2015.

$100 between 1979 and 1985, at a time that the comparable wage in the cities that made up the Card placebo fell by only $50.

This difference, in fact, downplays the true impact of Mariel, because the placebo cities that Card chose do not form a true placebo at all. Card describes his selection process as follows:

[The placebo cities] were selected both because they had relatively large populations of blacks and Hispanics and because *they exhibited a pattern of economic growth similar to that in Miami over the late 1970s and early 1980s.* A comparison of employment growth rates . . . suggests that economic conditions were very similar in Miami and the average of the four comparison cities *between 1976 and 1984.*[12]

Note that the four cities in Card's placebo were selected partly because they were similar to Miami *after* Mariel. This elementary error is akin to a medical researcher choosing the placebo by looking for patients who were not injected with a harmful dosage of an experimental drug but somehow got sick anyway.

A true placebo should contain cities that had similar rates of employment growth *before* Mariel. The cities in the "employment placebo" in Figure 7.4 (Anaheim, Rochester, Nassau-Suffolk, and San Jose) had rates of employment growth almost identical to those of Miami in the years prior to Mariel. It is obvious that choosing a correct placebo makes the post-Mariel situation of Miami's low-skill workforce look much worse.

In short, both the Mariel data and an examination of how wages have grown for different skill groups over the past few decades confirm that the laws of supply and demand work—even when it comes to immigration. Moreover, the effect is numerically important, with a 10 percent increase in supply lowering wages by 3–4 percent in the national labor market, and by at least 10 percent in the exceptional context of the Mariel supply shock.

4. ACCOUNTING FOR COMPLEMENTARITIES

THERE IS A problem with these estimates of the wage impact: they measure how a supply shock in a particular skill group affects native wages in *that* group, but those immigrants affect other groups as well.

Low-educated immigrants influence the wage of high-educated natives; young immigrants affect the productivity of older natives. And the wage gains from these complementarities could be substantial. The correct estimate of the wage effect of immigration should include those gains.

We would ideally like to measure the complementarities among all skill groups, but that makes the exercise intractable. For example, if immigration into each of the 40 age-education groups defined earlier affected the wage of every other group, there would be 1,600 potential wage effects to worry about.

And this is where economic theory comes in. There exist mathematical models of a hypothetical economy that make the problem manageable. However, what some would consider innocuous assumptions about the US economy or how widgets are manufactured, others might view as a straitjacket, a type of data "torturing." In fact, it is a bit of both. Some assumptions are needed, or we will never make progress on estimating 1,600 wage effects. But there is some data torturing too, because the hypothetical economy introduces many false assumptions about what the economy looks like and how widgets are produced.

Moreover, even if we were willing to simplify the problem along these lines, other researchers would rather make a *different* set of assumptions. Needless to say, different assumptions lead to different answers, creating a problem (or, should I say, an opportunity) in an issue as contentious as immigration. A cottage industry has developed in which researchers change assumptions and produce a wide array of answers. Those answers became the source for the "duels of expert opinion" cited in media and government reports throughout the recent debate over immigration reform.

My 2003 study introduced a hypothetical economy that made it "easy" to estimate the cross-effects. By streaming the real-world data scatter in Figure 7.3 through this prototype of the labor market, we can "see" what happens both in the short run, the morning after the helicopter drop, and the long run, after natives have fully adjusted to the supply shock.

Table 7.1 reports the predicted wage impact if all the immigrants

TABLE 7.1. PREDICTED IMPACT OF THE 1990–2010 SUPPLY SHOCK, ACCOUNTING FOR COMPLEMENTARITIES

Group	Increase in supply (percent)	Wage effect in short run (percent)	Wage effect in long run (percent)
High school dropouts	25.9	−6.2	−3.1
High school graduates	8.4	−2.7	0.4
Some college	6.1	−2.3	0.9
College graduates	10.9	−3.2	−0.1
Postcollege	15.0	−4.1	−0.9
All workers	10.6	−3.2	0.0

Source: George J. Borjas, *Immigration Economics* (Cambridge, MA: Harvard University Press, 2014), 114.

who entered the country between 1990 and 2010 were part of a single overnight helicopter drop. This supply shock was largest for the least and most educated workers. Not surprisingly, the morning-after (short-run) wage fell most for those two groups—by 6 percent for high school dropouts and by 4 percent for the most educated—even after taking the cross-group complementarities into account. If we average across all groups, the wage fell by 3 percent.

Before turning to the long-run effects, let me emphasize that the "long run" is an imaginary construct; it describes the hypothetical economy after all adjustments to the supply shock have taken place. For instance, the short-run drop in the wage increases profits, encouraging firms to expand and manufacture more of those profitable widgets. Because the model of the hypothetical economy precisely depicts how this economy works, we do not need to observe any of those adjustments. Nor do we need to know whether they take a month, a decade, or several decades to get done. We simply *imagine* all the adjustments happened, and the math does the rest.

Most strikingly, immigration has *zero* effect on the average wage in the long run—a statistic that received much attention in the debate. In 2013, the *National Journal* reported:

> Some of the most-cited research showing that immigration has depressed wages comes from a pair of Harvard economists, George Borjas and Lawrence Katz. . . . But zoom out a little and the effect is null: on average the long-term effect immigration had on wages from 1990 to 2010 was zero.[13]

Let me make a point about this misunderstood result as clearly as I can. *The predicted zero wage effect has nothing to do with the data.* It is *built in* by a technical assumption of the hypothetical economy: that the number of widgets produced would double if we could double labor and double capital (a property that economists call "constant returns to scale").* As Katz and I wrote in the study that introduced the long-run simulation: "It *must* be the case that the aggregate wage change must be identically equal to zero . . . because the production function . . . has constant returns to scale."[14]

With this assumption in hand, we would come up with the same zero effect if we looked at supply shocks in Canada, Singapore, or Kenya, or in the 1950s, the 1730s, or the year 2525. It is not, as the *National Journal* implied, that the data show that the "long-term effect immigration had on wages . . . was zero." It is instead that the prototype of the hypothetical economy *forced it to be zero*.

Because the average wage cannot change in the long run, some education groups must have had a wage cut, while others had a wage gain. As a result of the 1990–2010 supply shock, high school dropouts suffered the largest loss. Even in the long run, their wage fell by 3 percent.

High school dropouts make up a small share of the native popu-

---

* The model also builds in that the average short-run wage effect must equal the product of the share of income that accrues to capital (in the 1990–2010 context, about 0.3) and the percentage by which the supply increases (10.6 percent in this case).

lation; about 10 percent of native men do not have a high school degree. The average dropout earns about $29,000 a year, so a 3–6 percent wage effect implies a loss of $900–$1,700. These wage reductions are disproportionately borne by members of vulnerable groups; over a third of the dropouts are either African American or Hispanic.

The fact that immigration to the United States has often worsened the economic well-being of disadvantaged minorities was noted as early as 1855 by civil rights pioneer Frederick Douglass:

> The old employments by which we have heretofore gained our livelihood, are gradually, and it may seem inevitably, passing into other hands. Every hour sees the black man elbowed out of employment by some newly arrived immigrant whose hunger and whose color are thought to give him a better title to the place.[15]

Some observers, however, argue that we should not be too concerned with the losses suffered by low-skill Americans. As economist Bryan Caplan puts it:

> Are low-skilled Americans the master race? . . . Economists are used to rolling their eyes when people object to better policies on the grounds that some special interest will suffer from the change. It's time to cross the final frontier, and start rolling our eyes when the special interest is low-skilled Americans.[16]

My own view is that the economic, social, and political consequences of pursuing policies that harm the most disadvantaged Americans are ignored at our peril. It seems extremely shortsighted to dismiss the wage effect of immigration on low-skill workers by arguing that few workers are affected in this fashion or that, in any case, low-skill Americans are not "the master race."

5. SAVING THE NARRATIVE

THE FACT THAT wages fall for the skill groups that received the most immigrants—even after apparently accounting for all complementarities—makes it difficult to claim that immigration does not harm anyone. This deviation from the narrative inspired a lot of revisionist research. The decade-long effort identified two changes in the assumptions of the hypothetical economy that could restore the narrative. The first contends that immigrants and natives who seem to have identical skills are, in fact, complements. And the second asserts that high school dropouts and high school graduates are clones. Current claims that immigration has little impact on wages rely on research that makes these two assumptions. Both assumptions are wrong.

The hypothetical economy introduced in my 2003 study assumed that all "look-alike" workers are interchangeable; for example, all college graduates in their early thirties are productive clones. But what if a thirty-year-old college graduate from abroad was not a carbon copy of a thirty-year-old native-born college graduate? What if the immigrant knew things that he could pass on to his carbon-copy native? Then, immigrants would increase the productivity of even look-alike natives, and *everyone* would be better off.

It is far from clear that this type of carbon-copy complementarity is important in the real world. Most of us accept the idea that low-skill immigrants complement high-skill natives. But how exactly does a twenty-year-old *Marielito* make a twenty-year-old black dropout in Miami more productive?

The attempt to determine whether carbon-copy complementarities exist is associated mainly with economists Gianmarco Ottaviano and Giovanni Peri. The initial draft of their work, released as an unpublished paper in 2006, claimed that these complementarities were empirically important, so that immigration would indeed increase the wage of practically all natives.[17]

For a Bush administration peddling amnesty for undocumented

immigrants, the timing could not have been more fortuitous. The Bush-appointed economists at the Council of Economic Advisers wasted no time promoting the unpublished study:

> A recent paper by Ottaviano and Peri . . . concludes that immigration since 1990 has boosted the average wage of natives by between 0.7% and 1.8%. . . . Fully 90% of US native-born workers are estimated to have gained from immigration. Multiplying the average percentage gains by the total wages of US natives suggests that annual wage gains from immigration are between $30 billion and $80 billion.[18]

There was one slight problem with this rush to judgment. The Ottaviano-Peri claim depended on the mistaken classification of millions of native high school juniors and seniors as "high school dropouts," simply because those students did not yet have a high school diploma. After these so-called dropouts were excluded from the sample, the much-hyped (and politically useful) finding that look-alike immigrants and natives were complements vanished entirely.[19]

At the time, I tried reproducing some of the statistics in the CEA report but could not figure out how they were obtained. I was suspicious, but maybe the CEA staff knew something I should learn about. On June 20, 2007, I e-mailed the then-chief economist at the CEA, asking: "Is it possible to obtain more detail on how the CEA calculated the gains numbers from the Ottaviano-Peri elasticities. What formulas did you use? What numbers did you plug in?" Months later I received an answer: the chief economist had been unable, he said, to get approval to send me details about the calculations. My lifelong skepticism for claims made by politically motivated experts was vindicated yet again.

A revised version of the Ottaviano-Peri study was finally published in 2012.[20] The complementarities reported in the published article are far weaker than those claimed in the original draft, leading a recent survey to conclude that carbon-copy complementarities are, at best, "very modest."[21] Table 7.2 shows the wage effects under alternative sce-

TABLE 7.2. PREDICTED IMPACT OF THE 1990–2010 SUPPLY SHOCK ON NATIVE HIGH SCHOOL DROPOUTS, USING ALTERNATIVE SCENARIOS

	Effect on wages (percent)		
	Basic simulation	Allowing for carbon-copy complementarity	Also assuming that high school dropouts and graduates are productive clones
Short run	−6.2	−4.9	−2.1
Long run	−3.1	−1.7	1.1

Source: George J. Borjas, *Immigration Economics* (Cambridge: Harvard University Press, 2014), 120, 126.

narios. If we just allow for carbon-copy complementarity, native high school dropouts still suffered a 2–5 percent wage loss. Nevertheless, "complementarity" is now a buzzword bandied about by advocates who seem unaware of the huge difference between the flawed draft that made the political splash and the published version.*

Although carbon-copy complementarities failed to restore the narrative, *adding in* a second revisionist assumption, first introduced by David Card, gets rid of the vexing detail that low-skill Americans lose.[22] What if we defined the low-skill workforce differently? High school dropouts and high school graduates are usually assumed *not* to be clones of each other. But what if they were?

If high school dropouts and graduates were productive clones, the finding that immigrants hurt low-skill workers would mostly vanish. Table 7.2 shows that by "tucking away" high school dropouts inside

---

* In fact, even the "very modest" carbon-copy complementarities would disappear completely if Ottaviano and Peri had used more conventional statistical methods. See George J. Borjas, Jeffrey Grogger, and Gordon H. Hanson, "On Estimating Elasticities of Substitution," *Journal of the European Economic Association* 10 (2012).

a *much larger* low-skill workforce, the impact on the dropouts gets diluted and immigration barely changes the wage of the most disadvantaged workers.

The question, of course, is whether such an aggregation of workers is justified. And, again, the Mariel evidence shows that such an aggregation makes little sense. Figure 7.5 illustrates how the wage of both high school dropouts and high school graduates in Miami varied before and after Mariel. If the two groups were productive clones, we would expect similar trends; the Mariel supply shock should have adversely affected both groups of workers. In fact, the *Marielitos* sub-

FIGURE 7.5. EARNINGS OF HIGH SCHOOL DROPOUTS AND HIGH SCHOOL GRADUATES IN MIAMI

Average weekly earnings are calculated in a sample of non-Hispanic men aged twenty-five to fifty-nine. The data are smoothed using a three-year moving average.

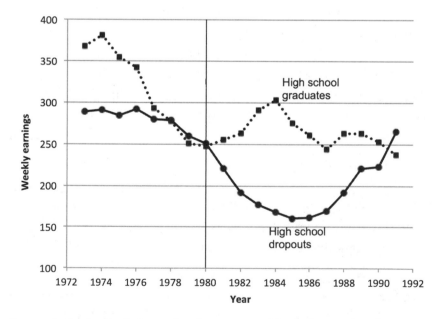

Source: Author's calculations using the 1972–1992 March Current Population Surveys.

stantially reduced the wage of high school dropouts and did not reduce the wage of high school graduates.

It is worth noting the cognitive dissonance in the two assumptions used to save the narrative: (1) look-alike immigrants and natives are complements, and (2) high school dropouts and high school graduates are clones. Put differently, workers that most of us view as different (high school dropouts and high school graduates) are identical, while workers that many might view as identical (carbon-copy workers with the same age and education) are different.

It is also telling that the saving-the-narrative game took the direction of hiding small groups in a larger whole—for example, pooling high school dropouts and high school graduates into a very big low-skill workforce. The aggregation dilutes the disparate impact suffered by the small group. This hide-and-*not*-seek game is misguided. If nothing else, the difference between the original Mariel study and my reappraisal written twenty-five years later shows the importance of specifically isolating the group of workers most likely to be affected by supply shocks.

Suppose we imported 50,000 sociologists with doctoral degrees. Such a supply shock would have little effect on PhD economists or PhD chemists, but it certainly would affect the job prospects of sociologists. If we defined "high skill" as a group that included all workers with doctoral degrees, we would certainly miss the impact of this supply shock.

Recent studies provide two real-world examples. The first examines the importation of foreign nurses. In 2010, over half of the registered nurses in New York were foreign-born; in Boston, however, only 10 percent were. This supply shock had a substantial displacement effect on native nurses in the affected cities: "For every foreign nurse that migrates to a city, between 1 and 2 fewer native nurses are employed in the city."[23] Obviously, the displacement effects would have been impossible to uncover, had the researchers examined the impact of foreign nurses on the job opportunities of all college graduates.

The second study looks at the construction industry in Norway.[24]

Some jobs, such as electricians and plumbers, require licensing, while others, such as carpenters and painters, do not. The jobs that require licensing are sheltered from a supply shock because immigrants often lack the correct credentials. Not surprisingly, immigration into the Norwegian construction industry had very different effects on the two types of jobs. A 10 percent supply shock reduced wages in the unsheltered jobs by 6 percent—relative to what happened in the jobs that required licensing. This wage effect would have been greatly diluted if all construction workers had been merged into a single group.

I have recounted how the saving-the-narrative research in the past decade tried to come up with alternatives to the assumptions introduced in my 2003 study. I also noted how the writing of We Wanted Workers inspired me to revisit Mariel, leading to the discovery that low-skill workers in Miami were indeed made worse off by the Marielitos.

It took much less time to address that deviation from the narrative. Within three months, after the public release of my Mariel study, counterattacks had been launched to restore order to the galaxy. For example, Giovanni Peri and Vasil Yasenov claimed that the narrative remained untouched if one recalculated the wage trends in Miami and the placebos using a different sample of workers.[25] I examined the impact of the Marielitos by looking at the earnings of non-Hispanic men aged twenty-five to fifty-nine; the men in this sample, which approximated the prime-age, native-born workforce, had already finished school and had not yet begun their retirement. The attempt to restore the narrative looked at all workers aged sixteen to sixty-one.

Remarkably, by adding teenagers aged sixteen, seventeen, or eighteen to the sample, Peri made the same mistake in data construction for the second time. As in his original analysis of carbon-copy complementarities, all high school sophomores, juniors, and seniors were misclassified as high school dropouts because they did not yet have a high school diploma. The earnings of these students come from part-time and summer jobs, so treating them as low-skill workers fatally distorts wage trends and makes it seem as if Miami was no different from any other place. In plain words: garbage in, garbage out.[26]

It is difficult to determine how and why such data manipulations enter and reenter the picture in attempts to restore the narrative. But it is peculiar that the sloppiness always leads to the same place: morphing the wage depression that did occur into a "finding" that nothing happened.

Paul Collier was the first to publicly note that social scientists would "strain every muscle" to ensure that published research indicated immigration was "good for everyone." Peri and Yasenov recommend expanding the exercise regime:

> We think the final goal of the economic profession should be to agree that . . . we do not find any significant evidence of a negative wage and employment effect of the Miami boatlift.[27]

Although there are countless other economic issues to worry about, the "economic profession" has its marching orders: reach the "final goal" of concluding that the *Marielitos* did not harm anyone. Such a call to arms reminds me very much of the Marxist-Leninist teachers at that revolutionary school in Havana long ago: *they believed*. All that was left was to compel everyone else to believe as well.

6. WHAT IS THE WAGE IMPACT?

PROTOTYPES OF HYPOTHETICAL economies are extremely useful: they help us think about a difficult problem, they isolate the issues that need to be addressed, they force researchers to be rigorous and write down assumptions, and they give a sense of the possible effects. Most economists are also keenly aware of the limitations of these prototypes. In fact, we spend a lot of time arguing about what we can learn from such exercises.

Unfortunately, the models are easy to misinterpret and misuse, particularly by advocates who are often clueless about what lies inside the black box. In addition, the impressive-looking algebra offers the veneer of scientific authority to anyone willing to manipulate the assumptions to get a desired result.

In my view, the most credible evidence on the labor market impact of immigration comes from studies that do *not* rely on models of hypothetical economies. Despite the many data problems that real-world studies often encounter, at least that evidence is not tainted by assumptions that offer tempting opportunities to manipulate the data and weave a narrative. The historical relation between the wages of specific skill groups and immigration into those groups summarizes what we know for sure: the earnings of the groups most affected by immigration grow at a slower rate.

A sensible inference from the actual data, based on either a decades-long tracking of specific skill groups or the Mariel supply shock, is that a skill group hit by a 10 percent increase in the number of workers probably faces a wage reduction of at least 3 percent, and perhaps even 10 percent if the unique Mariel experience could be generalized to the entire labor market. In the modern American context, this fact suggests that low-skill workers have paid much of the bill for whatever gains have accrued elsewhere. As with tainted sports records, the results from all subsequent theory-based games should bear an asterisk next to the statistic.

8

The Economic Benefits

RECEIVING COUNTRIES TYPICALLY support immigration for a simple reason: they perceive that immigrants generate an overall benefit for natives. If this perception were different, if it were believed that immigrants made natives worse off, there is ample historical evidence that the open doors would quickly close.

Some of the benefits come from the complementarities between immigrants and natives. Immigrants may make some natives more productive or may increase the profits of native-owned firms. Some benefits arise because immigration reduces the price of specific goods and services. The large low-skill immigration into California surely made it cheaper for Californians to have their homes cleaned and their lawns mowed. Some of the benefits result from the fact that immigrants are also consumers, increasing the demand for whatever natives produce. And immigrants themselves open up firms and create additional jobs, generating even more benefits.

The benefits could increase exponentially if the supply shock contained many exceptional persons. There is no doubt that high-skill immigration accelerates innovation. Over 40 percent of all Fortune 500 companies in 2010 were founded by immigrants or by the children of immigrants. Three-quarters of patents from top universities in 2011 had a foreign-born inventor. And immigrants account for a large share of Nobel Prizes: 33 percent in chemistry; 26 percent in economics; and 34 percent in physics and medicine.[1]

Given this track record, it is not surprising to hear assertions that immigrants account for a very large portion of economic output. The George W. Bush Institute claims that if the country had pursued a "pro-growth immigration policy" starting in the 1960s, GDP today would be about $2 trillion larger. Looking forward, the Bipartisan Policy Center predicts that enacting comprehensive immigration reform now would increase GDP by about $1 trillion twenty years hence. Even modest proposals, like legalizing the status of the DREAMers, the immigrants who moved to the United States illegally as children, are predicted to generate huge benefits. The Center for American Progress reports that such legalization, affecting only 2 million persons, would increase GDP by $330 billion (a gain of $165,000 per DREAMer).[2]

Whether these claims are correct depends entirely on the details, and by now we should not be shocked to learn that different methods can easily generate radically different estimates of the gains. After all, to accurately measure the gains from immigration, one needs to list all the possible channels through which immigration transforms the economy: how immigration changes wages, prices, and profits; how immigration changes the number of jobs in each sector; how native workers and native-owned firms respond.

Needless to say, this exhaustive calculation has *never* been done. Instead, the typical estimate of the gains relies on a model of a hypo-thetical economy that helps us visualize what happens when the labor market is flooded by millions of new workers, letting us record the ripple effects of immigration on all sectors. Put bluntly, *all* estimates of the economic benefits from immigration come from someone writ-ing down a few equations that purportedly describe how the economy works and then plugging in some numbers.

One important lesson from this theory-based exercise is that the "textbook" model of the labor market—the model that describes the commonsense laws of supply and demand—does indeed predict that immigrant participation in the productive life of our country increases the aggregate wealth of the native population. There *are* economic incentives for keeping the door open.

However, that model also predicts that the net gains for natives are modest—not in the trillions of dollars, not even in the hundreds of billions, but only about $50 billion annually. And the exercise reveals that if one is willing to parade this modest gain in policy discussions, then one must also be willing to parade other, less welcome, implications of the same calculation: immigration is responsible for a huge redistribution of wealth, totaling about a half-trillion dollars, from native workers who compete with immigrants to natives who use or employ immigrant labor.

These estimates seem inconsistent with the widespread belief that some immigrants—particularly high-skill immigrants—create substantial economic gains. To allow for the possibility of such gains, we need to deviate from the standard way we think about the labor market in one crucial aspect: we need to argue that high-skill immigration introduces ideas that "rub off" on the native population, increasing native productivity and wealth. Although there is some indication that such spillovers exist, the evidence is limited to very narrow contexts. In fact, the spillovers can be convincingly detected only when the immigrants are truly exceptional workers, such as those who would be on the short list of potential Nobel Prize winners, and when the natives are working closely with the foreign-born luminaries.

1. WHO GAINS AND BY HOW MUCH?

THE DEBATE OVER the wage effects of immigration is driven by the concern that immigration makes some native groups worse off. It is politically useful to argue that these wage effects are small or nonexistent if the goal is to admit more immigrants, or to claim that they are large and inequitable if the goal is to restrict immigration.

There is, however, another equally important reason for us to care about the wage impact: *somebody's lower wage is somebody else's higher profit.* The gains from the lower cost of labor accrue to everyone who uses those workers: large hotel chains hiring cheap laborers; families looking for help to run the household; consumers buying the goods and services that the immigrants and their native counterparts produce. As with free trade, the laws of supply and demand imply that the dollar gains accruing to the natives who gain *must be* numerically larger than the dollar losses suffered by the natives who lose. On the whole, therefore, immigration increases the wealth of natives, and the difference between what the winners win and the losers lose is called the "immigration surplus."

It is worth emphasizing that the distributional pain is the flip side of the economic gain. And, ironically, *the greater the distributional pain, the greater the economic gain.* It makes no sense—at least in the way we typically think about the labor market—to argue that there are no wage effects while simultaneously claiming that immigrants increase native wealth by billions or trillions of dollars. It also makes no sense to argue that immigrants greatly depress native wages while maintaining that there are no economic benefits to be had.

In an ideal world, we would measure the immigration surplus by making a *very* long list of all the ways in which immigration transforms the economy. We could then go through the list, item by item, and figure out what the economy would look like if the country had not admitted any immigrants. The difference between this counterfactual accounting and what actually happened would measure the increase in wealth due to immigration. We would also be able to figure out how much of the increased wealth went to natives and how much went to immigrants in return for their work.

But we do not live in this ideal world, so it is impossible to tally up in this way. By now, it should not be surprising that economists take the shortcut of replacing the comprehensive tally with a mathematical model of how a hypothetical economy works and how the various sectors fit together. After writing down the equations that describe this economy, we plug in numbers and, presto, the math spits out an estimate of the economic gains.

My first attempt to estimate the size of the immigration surplus came in 1991. Economist David Henderson asked me to contribute an article to the *Fortune Encyclopedia of Economics* that he was editing and suggested it would be interesting to include a couple of sentences discussing this number.

I have to admit that I originally thought this exercise would not be very useful and would be met with some derision simply because the predicted surplus is so far removed from the detailed accounting we would do if we had ideal data. To my surprise, some colleagues seemed intrigued by the calculations whenever I mentioned them. A few years later, I had the opportunity to expand the initial idea when Alan Krueger, who was then an editor of the *Journal of Economic Perspectives*, asked me to organize an immigration symposium for that journal. I produced an article that summarized what the textbook model of the labor market tells us about the immigration surplus.[3]

One key number needs to be plugged into the prototype of the hypothetical economy to figure out the surplus: By how much does the native wage go down when immigrants enter the labor market? Despite all the disagreements on wage effects discussed in the previous chapter, the exercise typically assumes that a 10 percent increase in supply reduces the wage of natives by 3 percent in the short run. In 2015, about 16 percent of the workforce was foreign-born, and GDP was about $18 trillion. The implied short-run immigration surplus then totals $50 billion annually (see Table 8.1).

This estimate depends on the many assumptions built into the hypothetical economy. Nevertheless, the exercise says something both useful and surprising: it is mathematically impossible for this widely used framework to spit out a huge number for the immigration surplus. A $50 billion surplus in the context of an $18 trillion economy is not that big a deal; it is less than three-tenths of 1 percent of GDP.

The calculation also reveals that this small surplus conceals a large redistribution of wealth. Native workers lose $516 billion, while native-

---

TABLE 8.1. THE SHORT-RUN IMMIGRATION SURPLUS, 2015

	Billions of dollars
Immigration surplus	50.2
Loss to native workers	515.7
Gain to native firms	565.9
Total increase in GDP	2,104.0
Payments to immigrants	2,053.8

Source: Updated from George J. Borjas, "The Economic Benefits from Immigration," *Journal of Economic Perspectives* (1995). The calculations assume that the immigrant share of the workforce is 16.3 percent and that GDP is $18 trillion.

---

owned firms gain $566 billion. If one wishes to believe that natives, on the whole, benefit from immigration and that the surplus is about $50 billion, it follows from the same calculation that native workers are sending a half-trillion-dollar check to their employers.[*]

As I noted earlier, I originally thought this exercise would be met with a big yawn because the approach is so far removed from reality. It is hard to describe my surprise (utter shock really) when I opened a letter from an advocacy group that was citing some of those numbers to raise funds for its organization. I suppose this type of thing happens all the time, but it certainly puts things in a very different perspective when *you* happen to be the source of those numbers and know precisely their limitations.

It is important to emphasize that this calculation describes what happens to the size and split of the native "economic pie" the morning after the helicopter drop. Over time, the increased profits encourage the proverbial widget factory to expand and flood the market with

---

[*] The calculation assumes that immigrants and natives are productive clones. The surplus, however, would still be less than $50 billion if we took productivity differences between the two groups into account.

more widgets until the excess profits disappear. Because immigration does not change either the average wage or the firm's profits in the long run, native workers and native employers neither gain nor lose. In the long run, the immigration surplus must be exactly equal to zero dollars.

It seems easy to imagine that adding millions of new people would create all kinds of economies of scale that would generate substantial gains, enriching everyone in the process. It also seems easy to imagine that adding all those millions would create diseconomies of scale, perhaps because of overcrowding or environmental consequences, impoverishing everyone along the way. Maybe one of those daydreams is true, but that is not the way the textbook model of the labor market is "cooked up." Just as the zero long-run wage effect discussed in the previous chapter was the result of a mathematical assumption (that doubling workers and doubling capital in the widget factory doubles the number of widgets produced), the same assumption ensures that the long-run immigration surplus is zero. Ironically, advocates who emphasize the zero wage effect in the long run are implicitly admitting that natives do not gain from immigration *at all*.

Despite the very small gains in the short run, and the nonexistent gains in the long run, there are many extravagant claims that immigration increases wealth by hundreds of billions or trillions of dollars. Those who make such claims get away with it because they often use a misleading notion of exactly what they mean by "gains." The immigration surplus measures the additional wealth that accrues to *natives*. This statistic is obviously not the same as the actual increase in GDP, since immigrants receive part of that increase as payment for their work.

As Table 8.1 shows, the current level of immigration in the United States generated a $2.1 trillion increase in GDP. But the immigrants themselves get paid about 98 percent of this increase; very little of it trickles down to natives. It is important to note, however, that immigrants gain substantially. The wage payments to immigrants (just over $2 trillion) far exceed what their income would have been, had they not migrated.

2. HIGH-SKILL IMMIGRATION

AS LONG AS we stick to the usual way of thinking about the labor market, immigration does not make natives much wealthier. We need to make one crucial change in the textbook model to predict huge gains—a change that would enable high-skill immigrants to raise productivity, speed up innovation, and contribute to economic growth in some other way.

Specifically, what if high-skill immigrants generated *beneficial* productivity spillovers? The story is simple: high-skill immigrants may expose natives to new types of expertise and knowledge, making native workers far more productive.

A lot of recent research attempts to detect the presence of such spillovers, trying to find empirical proof for the speculation that native workers become more productive when they hang out with high-skill immigrants. The search has focused on specific historical events that generated high-skill supply shocks both in the United States and abroad. Overall, the evidence indicates that high-skill immigration can indeed generate beneficial spillovers. However, the spillovers are easiest to find when the high-skill immigrants have exceptional talents, and when the spillover recipients work closely with the immigrants. Once we move away from this very unusual type of high-skill immigration, it becomes much more difficult to detect the spillovers.

Jewish Scientists in Nazi Germany

The work of economist Fabian Waldinger represents a pioneering example in the ongoing search for high-skill productivity spillovers.[4] In 1933, soon after Adolf Hitler secured power, the Nazi government enacted the notorious Law for the Restoration of the Professional Civil Service. A key provision of the law said: "Civil servants who are not of Aryan descent are to be placed in retirement." Because most university professors were civil servants, German universities dismissed their

Jewish faculty. For example, nearly 18 percent of mathematics professors were dismissed in 1933 and 1934.

At the time, German mathematics played a central role in the world mathematical community, so many of the dismissed professors had little trouble finding employment abroad. Waldinger used this supply shock to determine whether the sudden banishment of the Jewish professors affected the productivity of the doctoral students left behind in the most affected mathematics departments.

The two leading departments were those at the University of Göttingen and the University of Berlin. The professors dismissed from those departments included such eminent mathematicians as Richard Courant (who moved to New York University), Richard von Mises (Harvard), and John von Neumann (Princeton). In general, the best mathematics departments in Germany were the ones hardest hit.

Waldinger compared the careers of doctoral students who were enrolled in German universities before and after the dismissals. Not surprisingly, the doctoral students graduating from departments populated by the likes of Courant, von Mises, and von Neumann had a much larger probability of producing work that would be cited by other researchers before 1933 (see Figure 8.1). This advantage, however, disappeared soon after the Nazi dismissals.

The link between student accomplishment and the quality of the professors suggests the presence of beneficial spillovers. The departure of Jewish mathematical luminaries depressed the future output of students, who were deprived of that valuable mentorship.

In subsequent work, however, Waldinger extended the analysis to other scientific disciplines, including physics, and examined what happened to the *colleagues* of the dismissed Jewish faculty (rather than the students).[5] About 14 percent of German physics professors were also dismissed, including Albert Einstein. It turns out that the peers did not suffer at all from the dismissals; the publication rate of the colleagues of Albert Einstein and other dismissed Jewish physicists was unaffected.

This fascinating natural experiment provides what is probably the

FIGURE 8.1. THE PRODUCTIVITY OF GRADUATE STUDENTS AND THE DISMISSAL OF JEWISH MATHEMATICIANS

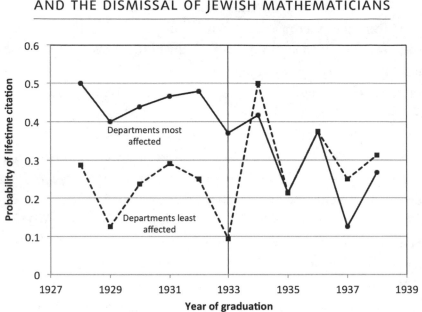

Source: Fabian Waldinger, "Quality Matters: The Expulsion of Professors and the Consequences for Ph.D. Student Outcomes in Nazi Germany," *Journal of Political Economy* 118 (2010): 813.

most convincing evidence that *very* high-skill supply shocks can generate beneficial productivity spillovers. But it also reveals that such spillovers do not happen automatically. The high-skill movers generate strong spillovers on the persons with whom they directly interact (that is, the students they mentor), but have much less impact on their "grown-up" colleagues, who now face less competition for resources.

The Collapse of the Soviet Union

Throughout much of Soviet history, Soviet scientists were prohibited from traveling to the West, contacting their Western colleagues, and freely exchanging ideas. After the collapse of the USSR, former Soviet scientists suddenly had the opportunity to travel and to apply for jobs in Western institutions. Many scientists, including many mathematicians, took advantage of this opportunity, generating an exodus of high-skill workers to Western countries.

The mathematics context is particularly interesting because a key historical event, now known as the "Luzin affair," cemented the separation of mathematicians on the two sides of the Iron Curtain. In 1936, Nikolai Luzin, a renowned mathematician at Moscow State University and a member of the USSR Academy of Sciences, became the target of a Stalinist witch hunt. He was accused of promoting anti-Soviet propaganda and of saving his best theorems for publication in foreign outlets. Soviet mathematicians quickly got the message: they should publish only in Soviet journals.

This physical and intellectual separation created a chasm between mathematicians in the Soviet Union and in the West. The two groups began to specialize in very different fields within the discipline of mathematics. The two most popular Soviet fields were partial and ordinary differential equations, accounting for 18 percent of all Soviet publications. The two most popular American fields were statistics and operations research, accounting for 16 percent of all American publications.

Spurred by the collapse of the Communist regime in 1992, more than a thousand Soviet mathematicians (about 10 percent of the total) left the country. A third of the émigrés settled in the United States, and they represented the cream of the crop, being the most prolific authors of research papers. It would not be surprising if the sudden presence of such gifted mathematicians had productivity spillovers on their American counterparts. The *New York Times,* in fact, reported how a Harvard mathematician was able to solve a long-standing problem by interacting with the Soviets:

> Persi Diaconis, a mathematician at Harvard, said: "It's been fantastic. You just have a totally fresh set of insights and results." Dr. Diaconis said he recently asked [Soviet mathematician] Dr. Reshetikhin for help with a problem that had stumped him for 20 years. "I had asked everyone in America who had any chance of know-

ing" . . . No one could help. But . . . Soviet scientists had done a lot of work on such problems. "It was a whole new world I had access to," Dr. Diaconis said.[6]

However, a few hundred Soviet mathematicians looking for work came along with the new ideas. The *New York Times* also reported:

American scientists . . . are being peppered with letters and calls asking for invitations. . . . "I have run across a number of very distinguished Soviet mathematicians who have come here as visitors and spend their time going around the country and looking for a job."[7]

Data collected by the American Mathematical Society (AMS) showed a sharp increase in the unemployment rate of newly minted mathematicians and identified "increased numbers of highly qualified recent U.S. immigrants seeking employment in the market for mathematical scientists" as a leading cause of the unprecedented 12 percent unemployment rate.[8] In other words, the job opportunities of people who prove theorems for a living are subject to the same laws of supply and demand that apply to construction workers, taxi drivers, and laborers. The AMS data, in fact, suggest that employment conditions in the entry-level market did not return to normal for nearly a decade.

I have been interested in this particular supply shock for many years. When I moved to Harvard in the mid-1990s, my family settled in Lexington, a Boston suburb. Because of its location and the quality of its public school system, Lexington is populated by many academics connected with the area's colleges and universities.

At my son's Little League games and Cub Scout activities, I became friends with one of the fathers, who was a mathematician. He had obtained his doctoral degree from MIT and had published several math papers. He recounted the difficulty he had faced when looking for work at the time of the Soviet supply shock, and how he had been unable to get an academic job. My friend's experience made an impression, particularly because he was obviously very smart and talented. I mentally filed the anecdote as something that was worth looking into.

A decade later I was giving a lecture at the University of Notre Dame, and I met Kirk Doran, a young economist who was interested in immigration issues. Somehow the subject of high-skill immigration and mathematicians came up. I resurrected my story from years earlier, and it turned out that Doran was also aware of the situation, as he personally knew people affected in exactly the same way. By the end of our conversation, it was clear that this was an issue worth exploring.

We soon discovered that the AMS maintains a data archive that records every single research paper published by every single mathematician in the world, so we could track the careers of American mathematicians before and after the Soviet supply shock. We were given access to these data and measured the impact of the supply shock on two different groups of American mathematicians: those who specialized in "Soviet fields," like differential equations; and those who specialized in "American fields," like statistics.[9]

The supply shock should have had little spillover effect on the Americans who worked in American fields because the Soviets had done little work in those areas during the long separation. But the supply shock could have made Americans working in Soviet fields more productive. The Soviets had developed many tools in those areas—tools that were now newly available to the Americans.

As the *New York Times* reporting suggests, it was hard to predict how things would actually turn out. On the one hand, the spillovers could increase the productivity of American mathematicians working on differential equations, by teaching them things they did not know before. On the other hand, those same American mathematicians had to compete with the Soviet émigrés for jobs and publication space. If the supply shock was large enough, it might become difficult for the "targeted" Americans to get the types of academic jobs that would allow them to carry out publishable research.

Figure 8.2 shows what actually happened. Prior to 1990, the most exposed Americans (those who worked in Soviet fields) had a slight

FIGURE 8.2. AMERICAN MATHEMATICIANS AND THE
COLLAPSE OF THE SOVIET UNION

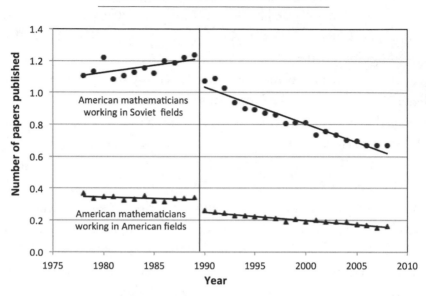

Source: George J. Borjas and Kirk B. Doran, "The Collapse of the Soviet Union
and the Productivity of American Mathematicians," *Quarterly Journal of Economics* 127 (2012): 1172.

upward trend in the number of papers published annually, while the
least exposed Americans (those who worked in American fields) had a
slight downward trend. After 1990, there was a precipitous decline in
the publication rate of the group whose research overlapped most with
the Soviets. Put simply, the American mathematicians who competed
most directly with the Soviet émigrés lost out.

The nature of the academic market explains how this can happen.
The number of mathematics research jobs in the United States was
roughly constant in the 1990s, so the entry of exceptional Soviet mathematicians crowded out newly minted mathematicians and untenured
faculty. Many of the displaced American mathematicians moved to
lower-ranked institutions or out of the academic market altogether.
That move made it difficult for them to do the type of research that
leads to publication, perhaps because of increased teaching loads or

because jobs in the private sector, such as a "quant" in Wall Street, limit the time one can devote to deriving publishable theorems. The academic market makes it very difficult for researchers with a hiatus in their research output to get back on the academic track, so the adverse effect of the supply shock was permanent for many of the affected Americans.

The noticeable impact of the Soviet supply shock helps reemphasize a key lesson about how we should define skill groups when trying to measure the impact of immigration. As we saw in the previous chapter, the aggregation of different types of workers into a larger whole helps to hide how supply shocks affect the targeted groups. The impact of the Soviet émigrés would be much harder to detect if we ignored the fact that different mathematicians do different types of work, and instead treated all mathematicians as a single group. Supply shocks often have laser-focused effects on very specific types of workers, and it is a mistake—even if it helps to preserve the narrative—to blend all those types.

The H-1B Program

The United States uses the H-1B visa program to grant temporary entry to high-skill immigrants in "specialty occupations." These occupations usually require specialized knowledge in science, engineering, or computer-related jobs. Not all the visas go to computer programmers, but the program is thought of as affecting mainly the high-tech industry.

The number of H-1B visas is capped. The cap has fluctuated over time and has been 65,000 visas per year since 2004. The policy debate revolves around whether the cap should be increased, with some advocates arguing that there should not be any cap at all. The claim that high-skill immigration generates beneficial productivity spillovers is often used to argue for the expansion of the program. Testifying before Congress, for example, Bill Gates claimed that Microsoft created four new jobs for each H-1B visa holder hired.[10]

The conclusion that the H-1B program is beneficial often comes from studies that compare the rate of innovation and the employment of high-tech workers across cities. Economists William Kerr and William Lincoln conducted the best-known study of this type. They observe that H-1B visa holders cluster in a small number of locations. For example, between 2001 and 2002, employers in the San Francisco area filed twice as many H-1B applications as those in Houston.[11]

The comparison of different cities after an increase in the cap shows a rise in patenting in cities where firms would be expected to apply for the H-1B visas (like San Francisco). Interestingly, the increased patenting comes mainly from persons with Indian or Chinese surnames, suggesting that those new patents flowed from the creativity of the visa holders themselves, rather than from a spillover effect on native workers.

Subsequent research that uses the cross-city approach reports even stronger innovation effects of the program, arguing that native patenting increases when H-1B visa holders enter the local market. A news report summarizes these optimistic findings as indicating that "foreign workers bring innovations with them which lead to new inventions, more jobs and higher wages."[12]

The evidence reported in some of these cross-city studies, however, is not credible. One well-known study, for example, estimates that a 10 percent increase in the size of the workforce would raise the wage of college graduates by an eye-popping 80 percent.[13] Let me rephrase this result in context. If we could just get Congress to print another 15 million H-1B visas, the wage of native-born college graduates would nearly double! One must have a financial stake in the H-1B program or be very gullible or be ideologically blind to take such a claim seriously.

The problem with the cross-city comparisons is easy to explain. The helicopter drop of H-1B visas in different cities is not random. Most likely, the new H-1Bs ended up in parts of the country where there were many H-1B visa holders already employed because there was something about that particular area that was conducive to the high-tech industry—for instance, Silicon Valley or the Boston 128 corridor. Put simply, correlation does not imply causation. The fact that natives patent more in places where there are more H-1B visas may simply indicate that

H-1B visa holders end up in cities that are "sizzling" and natives would have patented anyway, rather than indicating that the visa holders are somehow stirring the creativity of their native colleagues.

The most persuasive evaluation of the H-1B program to date examines the results of a peculiar lottery used to award the visas.[14] It turns out that firms can apply for the visas on a first-come, first-served basis until the visas run out. On some random day during a year, the visas run out and *on that day* more firms typically apply for visas than there are visas available. For example, there may be 238 visas left at 12:01 a.m. on May 26, but firms apply for 345 visas during the next twenty-four hours. The Department of Homeland Security then runs a lottery to determine which of the 345 applicants will get an H-1B slot. In other words, the helicopter takes off on its haphazard journey and begins to deliver the scarce H-1B visas at random.

If the productivity spillovers were powerful, or if the H-1B visa holders were superb innovators, we would expect to find that the firms that won the lottery eventually patented more and that employment in those firms either increased or remained stable. It turns out that neither of those things happened. The firms that won the lottery did not patent more, and native employment in those firms fell. In fact, the evidence suggests that each H-1B visa holder crowded out one native worker. It is unclear, however, if this experimental evidence can be generalized to the entire program, because the firms that wait until the visas are almost exhausted might differ from the firms that jump at the first opportunity to apply for one of the coveted slots.

A 2015 *New York Times* report vividly describes how the crowd-out works and how US employers abuse the H-1B program:

> About 250 Disney employees were told . . . that they would be laid off. Many of their jobs were transferred to immigrants on temporary visas for highly skilled technical workers, who were brought in by an outsourcing firm based in India. Over the next three months, some Disney employees were required to train their replacements to do the jobs they had lost. "I just couldn't believe they could fly

people in to sit at our desks and take over our jobs exactly," said one former worker. . . . "It was so humiliating to train somebody else to take over your job. I still can't grasp it."[5]

In short, the evidence supporting the claim that the H-1B program has beneficial spillover effects is, at best, mixed. Studies that claim to find spillovers may just be showing that H-1B visa recipients end up in cities where the high-tech market is booming and native patenting is already high. If we look at what happens when the visas are assigned randomly to firms—so as to better replicate the conditions of the helicopter parable—there is little evidence of additional innovation and some evidence of job displacement. All the wishful thinking about high-skill immigration cannot overcome the fact that the data do not always cooperate.

High-skill immigration imparts huge benefits on natives *only if* there are beneficial productivity spillovers—if some of the exceptional abilities of the high-skill immigrants rub off on native workers.

The evidence in favor of spillovers seems strongest when the high-skill immigrants have truly exceptional skills and when there is a close personal relationship between those who are part of the supply shock and those who are affected by the supply shock. The impact of the Nazi dismissal of Jewish scientists on the productivity of the students left behind is a classic example.

The evidence for spillovers becomes much weaker once we move away from that unique set of circumstances. The entry of a few hundred Soviet mathematicians into the American mathematical community likely generated spillovers, but those spillovers could not overcome the laws of supply and demand. The supply shock of Soviet mathematicians made it harder for their native counterparts to find and hold the types of jobs that allow mathematicians to have research careers. Similarly, the spillovers from the H-1B visa program, where the average skill of the 65,000 immigrants who make up the annual supply shock is far lower, have proved difficult to detect, and their detection has much to do with the approach used to detect them.

9

The Fiscal Impact

THE CONCEPTUAL CLASH between the two views of immigrants that I have emphasized—immigrants as workers or immigrants as people—takes a front-row seat when it comes to thinking about the fiscal impact of immigration. If immigrants were simply raw labor inputs that came to the United States only to work and generate economic value while on the production line, we would not have to worry about what happens outside the factory gates. They would be, after all, a type of robotic worker without needs that might implicate the welfare state, and they could be easily disposed of once their productive value was exhausted.

But immigrants are people, and the welfare state both administers to people's needs and is funded by those same people, introducing a big new wrinkle into the discussion. Immigrants do have lives outside the factory gates; they have children, go to the hospital, pay taxes, cannot pay the rent, and retire. Outside those gates, they run into a wide array of government programs designed to ease the path through what can be very difficult times.

Given this reality, it should not be surprising that the concern about immigrants spills over to their fiscal impact. How do immigrants affect expenditures on the programs that make up the welfare state? And how do those expenditures compare to the taxes immigrants pay and the economic benefits they create during their time on the assembly line?

The concern over the link between immigration and welfare actually begins before any immigrant arrives. One often hears that social insurance programs are a magnet for immigrants. The safety net in many industrialized countries, including the United States, allows a much more comfortable and secure life than would be provided by the typical job in many developing countries. The welfare state might then attract persons who otherwise might not have migrated. Moreover, the magnetic attraction does not end after the move. The safety net may also discourage immigrants who "fail" in the United States from returning home.

Although it has proved very difficult to quantify these magnetic effects, there is little doubt that incentives matter in all aspects of life. And the welfare state does change the set of incentives that enter the immigration decision. The question, therefore, is not whether such magnetic effects exist. The question is instead: How strong are they?

Milton Friedman made a famous quip that encapsulates the concern. Despite his impeccable free-market credentials, Friedman said: "It's just obvious you can't have free immigration and a welfare state."[1] Friedman, in fact, went on to emphasize that the welfare state had to come into the picture when trying to come up with a sensible way of thinking about immigration:

> There is no doubt that free and open immigration is the right policy in a libertarian state, but in a welfare state it is a different story: the supply of immigrants will become infinite. Your proposal that someone only be able to come for employment is a good one but it would not solve the problem completely. The real hitch is in denying social benefits to the immigrants who are here. . . . Look, for example, at the obvious, immediate, practical example of illegal Mexican immigration. Now, that Mexican immigration . . . is a good thing. It's a good thing for the illegal immigrants. It's a good

thing for the United States. It's a good thing for the citizens of the country. But, it's only good so long as it's illegal.[2]

Note that Friedman stressed the crucial distinction between workers and people: It would be great if the only immigrants admitted were those who come for employment, but "the real hitch is in denying social benefits to the immigrants who are here." Friedman then chose the interesting example of undocumented Mexicans to emphasize the point. The economic gains that accrue to the United States are a "good thing" only if we can bar undocumented immigrants from access to social benefits. In short, illegal immigration is *only good so long as it's illegal.*

The fact that we need to contend with the workers-people distinction has cornered some libertarians into arguing that the problem is not immigration, but the existence of the welfare state in the first place. As William Niskanen, a former chairman of the Cato Institute, put it: "Better to build a wall around the welfare state than the country."[3]

Some things, however, are easier said than done. And if the real-world data that I will summarize in this chapter are any indication, the wall built around our welfare state does not appear to prevent many immigrants from entering that particular territory. The statutes that make up that wall *already* specify that any individual who is likely at any time to become a public charge is not admissible, and allow for the deportation of immigrants who become public charges within five years of entry. Moreover, the welfare reform enacted in 1996 prohibits most new immigrants from receiving federal assistance, with the ban being lifted when the immigrant becomes a US citizen (a process that takes at least five years).

As we shall see, Milton Friedman's concerns were well founded. Despite the many restrictions on welfare use by immigrants, the evidence indicates that immigrant households are far more likely to receive assistance than are native households. Given the obvious fact that immigrants do indeed receive services, the discussion has evolved into a contentious debate over whether immigrants pay their way.

They might use services, but perhaps the cost of those services is covered by the taxes they contribute.

The determination of whether immigrants pay their way is based on a seemingly simple exercise. On the one hand, we add up all the taxes immigrants pay, including income taxes, sales taxes, and property taxes. On the other hand, we figure out how much it costs to provide services to the immigrant population, including welfare, public schools, police and fire protection, and building additional roads to serve a larger population.

Inevitably, there are many different interpretations of what the data actually say, turning the debate into a battle of dueling experts who use different methodologies and assumptions to reach different answers.

CNN, 2014:

A Congressional Budget Office report . . . concluded that a path to legalization for immigrants would increase federal revenues by $48 billion. Such a plan would see $23 billion in increased costs from the use of public services, but ultimately, it would produce a surplus of $25 billion for government coffers.[4]

Federation for American Immigration Reform, 2011:

Illegal immigration costs U.S. taxpayers about $113 billion a year at the federal, state and local level. The bulk of the costs—some $84 billion—are absorbed by state and local governments.[5]

The exercise becomes much tougher if we want to measure the fiscal impact over the long run. The fertility rate of American women is well below the replacement rate, making it impossible to pay off the unfunded liabilities in such programs as Social Security and Medicare. At some point, the day of reckoning will require a substantial increase in taxes or a substantial cut in benefits (or both). Immigration can increase the number of taxpayers, helping to spread the future burden. The predicted fiscal impact of immigration will then depend on many factors that are unknowable at present, including the future rate of economic growth, as well as the future path of taxes and government expenditures.

Despite all the confusion, there is a simple arithmetic fact about the welfare state that is worth keeping in mind: *By design,* the welfare state subsidizes persons who have below-average incomes, and those subsidies are paid for by persons who have above-average incomes. In a nutshell, the welfare state redistributes income from the well-off to the disadvantaged.

If the typical immigrant was a high-skill person, outperforming others in the labor market, that immigrant would surely be defraying the cost of welfare programs. But if the typical immigrant was a low-skill person, performing worse than other workers, that immigrant would likely receive a net subsidy. Put bluntly, low-skill immigration is likely to be a drain on native taxpayers, while high-skill immigration is likely to be a boon. This simple "iron law of welfare" is often lost behind the political confusion and deliberate obfuscation in the immigration debate.

1. WELFARE USE BY IMMIGRANTS

A RECURRING THEME in this book has been that it is important to look at the nuts and bolts of how we learn certain things about immigration. As we have seen, sometimes the data are tortured a bit too much to trust the conclusion, and sometimes the conclusion is actually built in by the assumptions.

Looking under the hood is particularly important when asking if immigrants are net contributors to or net users of the programs in the welfare state. Yet again, the answer depends on what data are used, how the data are manipulated, and what assumptions are made.

The wide range of conclusions allows for a lot of cherry-picking by advocates. Depending on one's perspective, it is possible to cite a study claiming that immigrants use welfare a lot and impose a fiscal burden on natives, but it is also possible to cite an equally impressive-looking study claiming that natives benefit because immigrants contribute more to the treasury than they take out.

Given this disparity, it is enlightening to illustrate—in a very simple way—how the same publicly available data can support either one of the two polar viewpoints. The Current Population Survey (CPS) is the premier monthly survey of the US population and is collected by the Census Bureau. It is the survey used to calculate the official unemployment rate that makes news upon its release every first Friday of the month.

The March survey is particularly important for researchers. In addition to the monthly inquiries about employment and unemployment, the March survey solicits information on a person's income in the previous calendar year, and on whether the person received particular types of public assistance, including Medicaid, food stamps, and cash benefits. Since 1994, the CPS has reported whether a person is foreign-born, so we can now construct a twenty-year-long series on welfare use by immigrants and natives and see how those trends compare.

It is important to emphasize that the CPS data, like the decennial census, include all foreign-born persons who happen to be enumerated by the Census Bureau. The statistics that I will report here, therefore, include welfare use by both legal and undocumented immigrants, and it is not possible to ascertain which group is most responsible for the trends.

To keep things simple, being "on welfare" will mean receiving benefits from any one of three programs: Medicaid, food stamps, or cash benefits.* Many other programs could be thought of as some type of welfare, ranging from public housing to free school lunches. The frac-

---

* Cash benefits include Temporary Assistance for Needy Families (TANF), Supplemental Security Income (SSI), or "general" assistance given by cities and counties to persons in dire need.

tion of both natives and immigrants on welfare would obviously be higher if one were to include these additional programs, but it is easy to illustrate the main point by concentrating on the three main programs that make up the safety net. We are interested in finding out whether the fraction of immigrants on welfare is higher, lower, or the same as the fraction of natives on welfare.

The two "curtains" of Figure 9.1 show the twenty-year trends in welfare use calculated from the CPS, but for now I will not reveal the difference between the two curtains. Let me emphasize that I am using the same CPS data to calculate the trends in both curtains. Nevertheless, it is obvious that in curtain 1, immigrants are on welfare far more often than natives, and increasingly so. But in curtain 2, the welfare use of the two groups is essentially the same.

Let me reemphasize: *both curtains use exactly the same data.* Depending on our perspective, it is easy to cherry-pick the curtain that fits the desired ideological position and claim either that official government data show that immigrants use welfare much more often than natives and the gap is widening, or that official government data show that immigrants do not use welfare more often than natives. The

FIGURE 9.1. TRENDS IN WELFARE USE, 1994–2015

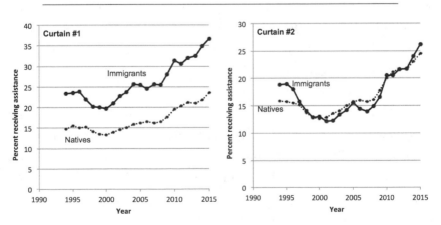

Source: Author's calculations using the 1994–2015 March Current Population Surveys.

one conclusion that the data do not allow is that immigrants use welfare less often than natives.

So, what is the difference between the two curtains? It all depends on the fine print. In curtain 1, I am reporting welfare use by *households*—which is the way welfare use is most often analyzed in social science research. Most welfare programs, after all, are allocated at the household level. For example, it is the presence of minor children that might entitle a single mother to receive an income grant for the family. In curtain 1, the CPS data are manipulated to determine whether anyone in the household receives Medicaid, food stamps, or cash.

An immigrant household is one in which the head of the household is foreign-born, and a native household is one in which the head is native-born. It is evident that households headed by an immigrant have particularly high rates of welfare use, and that the gap between immigrant and native households increased over time. By 2015, 37 percent of immigrant households were on welfare, compared to 24 percent of native households.

But the trends in curtain 2 seem to contradict this observation. In this alternative scenario, I manipulated the data so that the frame of reference is a single *person*, rather than a household. In other words, the relevant question becomes: Did a particular individual receive welfare? If one calculates the fraction of people who received assistance, there is little difference between immigrants and natives. About 25 percent of both groups received welfare in 2015.

What exactly is going on? I introduced a subtle trick in creating curtain 2. Suppose a young, single immigrant woman arrives in the United States. After a few years in the country, she becomes a single mother and has two children. In curtain 1, this three-person grouping is classified as an immigrant household. If the mother's income is sufficiently low, the children (and perhaps even the mother herself) qualify for some type of assistance. The household enters the tally *once*, as an immigrant household on welfare.

In curtain 2, this three-person household enters the tally three different times. If this household is on Medicaid, the tally records *one immigrant person* on welfare and *two native persons* on welfare. And therein lies the trick: because the children were born in the United States, they enter the cost-benefit calculation on the native side of the ledger. As the two curtains illustrate, this trick makes a huge difference in what conclusion we draw from the same data. To emphasize yet again, the fine print matters!

My own view is that the trends in curtain 2 are uninformative and misleading. The decision of whether or not to admit an immigrant should depend on the long-term implications of that decision, including the immigrants' choice of how many children to have and whether the government will have to fund the services provided to those dependents. The US-born children of immigrant households would not exist, and those welfare expenditures would not be incurred, if the immigrant was never admitted in the first place.

The distinction between curtains 1 and 2 might seem a purely academic exercise, unrelated to the public debate, but the editorial board of the *Wall Street Journal* helpfully served up a reminder in 2015 of how cherry-picking the data leads to the desired ideological point:

> The Center for Immigration Studies recently found "significantly higher welfare use associated with immigrants." But . . . they didn't measure individuals. To get to the headline-grabbing result, CIS had to measure households. Given that immigrant households are typically larger than those of native-born Americans, simple arithmetic means that the more people you have in a home, the more likely one of these people will receive . . . government benefit.[6]

The *Wall Street Journal* does not ask why exactly the immigrant household is larger. Nor does it point out that many of those extra people in the household would enter the tally as natives if the calculation were done at the person level.

Remarkably, we are not yet done with the data problems. In addition to the subtle manipulations involved in creating the two curtains in Figure 9.1, there exists another major problem with many of the welfare statistics thrown around in the political debate: the CPS, the source of many of those statistics, is notorious for providing poor measures of welfare use in the population—for both immigrants and natives.

The Survey of Income and Program Participation (SIPP), which is also conducted by the Census Bureau, is the "gold standard" on welfare use. The SIPP was specifically designed to get better measures of program participation, whereas the historical purpose of the CPS was to calculate the monthly unemployment rate. The SIPP has been shown to give much more reliable figures on welfare participation.[7]

The SIPP, however, is not as user-friendly as the CPS. It is *much* harder for a researcher to manipulate the SIPP data than to conduct the same exercise in the CPS. Not surprisingly, the typical study of welfare use by immigrants relies on data from the CPS, which is far from perfect, but far more convenient to use.

This research shortcut gives a *very* misleading picture of the difference between immigrants and natives. Table 9.1 reports the fraction of households on welfare in 2012 using both the CPS and the SIPP. The widely used CPS understates welfare use by both immigrants and natives, but the error is far greater for immigrants. According to the SIPP, 46 percent of immigrant households—*almost half*—were on welfare, compared to only 27 percent of native households.

Unfortunately, the SIPP does not report an immigrant's specific country of birth, so it is impossible to determine which groups are most responsible for such high welfare use. The SIPP, however, does report whether the household head is Hispanic or Asian. It is apparent that much of the excess use comes from Hispanic immigrant households. According to the SIPP, over 60 percent of such households received welfare in 2012, compared to only 30 percent for households headed by Asians or non-Hispanic whites.

The fact that immigrants use welfare more often than natives is striking, but not that surprising. The iron law of welfare programs— redistribution from the well-off to the disadvantaged—must imply

TABLE 9.1. WELFARE USE BY IMMIGRANTS
AND NATIVES IN 2012

	Households receiving welfare (percent)	
	CPS data	SIPP data
Natives	21.1	27.4
Immigrants	32.5	45.8
By race and ethnicity:		
Asian immigrants	20.0	30.5
Black immigrants	33.5	47.2
Hispanic immigrants	44.7	61.9
Non-Hispanic white immigrants	21.4	30.9

Source: Author's calculations using the 2013 Current Population Survey and the 2012 calendar-year waves of the Survey of Income and Program Participation.

that welfare recipients tend to be people who would do poorly in the labor market. Because the immigrant population is disproportionately low-skill, a disproportionately high number of welfare recipients are foreign-born.

In fact, ample evidence indicates that the main reason immigrants use welfare more often is not that they are immigrants, but that they are, on average, less skilled.[8] Half of the gap between the two groups would disappear if we simply compared the welfare use of similarly educated immigrants and natives. And about 70 percent of the gap would disappear if we also adjusted for differences in household size and state of residence. In other words, it is not "immigrant-ness" that is mainly responsible for the high welfare use by immigrant households. It is, instead, that these households are particularly vulnerable, and the available safety net protects them from very poor outcomes.

What *is* surprising is the very high level of welfare use among immigrants in general. It is difficult to remain unconcerned when 46 percent of immigrant households receive some type of public assistance.

2. THE NATIONAL ACADEMY OF SCIENCES

THE WELFARE STATE raises a multitude of questions about the economic, political, and cultural impact of immigration. How does welfare use affect the long-term assimilation of immigrants? What is the impact of the welfare state on political participation by immigrants? What are the implications of welfare dependency for the social fabric in immigrant communities?

Despite the importance of these questions for any overall assessment, the immigration debate has focused on a much simpler and presumably more easily answerable question: Do immigrants pay their way in the welfare state? In other words, do the taxes that immigrants pay cover the additional expenditures they trigger?

The array of conflicting answers to this question allows us to conclude whatever is ideologically convenient. To resolve the conflict in what seems to be an answerable question, the NAS was asked to examine the evidence in the mid-1990s and come up with an independent estimate of the bottom line. The hope was that this review would conclusively establish whether immigrants are a fiscal burden or a fiscal blessing.

The NAS gathered a panel of social scientists (including economists, sociologists, and demographers) to look at the existing evidence, perhaps improve on the methodology, and come up with an answer. The estimates in the NAS report published in 1997 became "conventional wisdom" and were referred to frequently in subsequent years.

Fast-forward a couple of decades and the NAS has gathered a new panel to reexamine the question and update the calculations.* It is extremely useful to provide a historical perspective of the NAS conclusions. Such a perspective gives us two decades' worth of hindsight to see

---

* Full disclosure: I was a member of both NAS panels.

how well the experts did back in 1997. Those lessons form a valuable reference point for interpreting the projections that the new panel makes.

The NAS panels estimated the fiscal impact of immigration both in the short run and in the long run. The short-run calculation is easy to explain. Suppose we look at the population in a particular state in a particular year. We can use the available data to calculate the cost of services provided to each person in the population that year. We can also use the income data to estimate how much each person paid in taxes. We can then add up the two columns, calculate the difference between the cost of services provided and taxes paid, and come up with an estimate of the bottom line.

The short-run estimates in the 1997 NAS report are essentially a tallying of this type done separately for the immigrant and native populations. The tally of the costs included all the usual welfare programs, as well as the cost of any additional services provided by state or local governments, ranging from public schools to garbage collection, and from incarceration to fire protection. The tally of taxes was also comprehensive, including income taxes, sales taxes, automobile taxes, alcohol taxes, and property taxes.

The 1997 panel carried out this short-run calculation for two states, California and New Jersey. Given the differences in earnings and welfare use between immigrants and natives, it is not surprising that the tally indicated that immigrants paid less in taxes and received more services. As a result, immigration turned out to be a fiscal burden, particularly in California, a state that offers generous services and has many low-skill immigrants. Extrapolating the experience of California and New Jersey nationwide implied that each native household paid about $300 per year (in inflation-adjusted 2015 dollars) to fund the services provided to immigrants back in 1997.[9]

Accounting for the much larger immigrant population today raises the per-native household cost to about $470 a year.* Because

---

* There were 9.9 million immigrant households and 89.7 million native households in 1996. The finding that immigration cost each native household $300 implies that

there are 106 million native households today, the total fiscal burden is about $50 billion annually. The 2016 NAS panel estimated that the burden would be even larger if we also accounted for the expansion in state-and-local government services since 1997. The fiscal burden would then rise to between $60 billion and $130 billion.* Put bluntly, immigration unambiguously imposes a fiscal burden on the native population in the short term.

There are, however, two conceptual difficulties with the point-in-time comparison between taxes paid and benefits received. Although some services, such as schooling for children, are costly to provide to immigrants today, they are also an investment, and this investment will generate fiscal benefits eventually. The children will have higher salaries, pay more in taxes, and require fewer services.

In addition, the short-run exercise ignores the fact that the aging of the native population will inevitably create fiscal problems in the future and that immigration can perhaps help alleviate those problems. The replacement fertility rate in the United States is about 2.1 children per woman, but the average native woman has only 1.8 children.[10] This fertility gap will make it impossible to fund many programs in the long term, unless benefits are drastically cut, taxes are dramatically increased, or *additional taxpayers are found*. A helicopter drop of millions of immigrants might just be the source of those taxpayers.

The 1997 NAS panel estimated the long-run fiscal impact of immigration by tracking what happens over the 300 years after the entry of a particular immigrant. Think of the sequence of events triggered by admitting an immigrant today: The country incurs some costs. Over

---

the total costs were $26.9 billion. There were 18.4 million immigrant households and 106.3 million native households in 2015, implying that the total cost due to the larger immigrant population was $50 billion, or $470 per native household.

* The 2016 panel also found that the estimated burden increases considerably (to perhaps $300 billion) if immigrants are charged for their share of federal expenditures; see Francine D. Blau and Christopher Mackie, eds., *The Economic and Fiscal Consequences of Immigration* (Washington, DC: National Academies Press, 2016), Tables 9-12a and 8-2.

TABLE 9.2. LONG-RUN FISCAL IMPACT OF THE
AVERAGE IMMIGRANT (1997 NAS REPORT)

Time span	Gain or loss
300 years	+$80,000
25 years	−$18,400
50 years	+$11,200
300 years and no budget adjustment in 2016	−$15,000

Source: James P. Smith and Barry Edmonston, eds., *The New Americans: Economic, Demographic, and Fiscal Effects of Immigration* (Washington, DC: National Academy Press, 1997), 334, 337. All estimates are in 1996 dollars.

time, the immigrant's tax contributions grow as assimilation takes place. Equally important, the immigrant has children. The education of the children may be costly, but they eventually pay taxes and receive fewer services. The children of immigrants have their own children, and the process begins anew.

As Table 9.2 shows, the panel concluded that admitting one immigrant will generate a net gain of $80,000 when added up over three centuries (equivalent to $122,000 in inflation-adjusted 2015 dollars). Despite the short-run fiscal burden, immigrants seem to be a very good deal when viewed from this longer-term perspective. The main reason is that more immigration means more taxpayers: "The role immigrants play in bearing the cost of the aging of the baby-boom generations and of rising health costs, largely for the elderly, contributes very strongly to their overall positive impact, more so than does any other single factor."[11]

Not surprisingly, the $80,000 estimate got a lot of media coverage at the time and continued to be widely cited for years afterward. For example, the Council of Economic Advisers in 2007, at the time that the Bush administration was trying to get Congress to enact amnesty for undocumented immigrants, resurrected the number by claiming that the long-run approach captures the full costs and benefits of the children of immigrants. Of course, such projections must rely on assumptions about the future path of taxes and government spending as well as economic and demographic trends. From this long-run point of view, the . . . study estimated that immigrants (including their descendants) would have a positive fiscal impact—a present discounted value of $80,000 per immigrant on average.[12]

There is no doubt that the long-run calculation is conceptually superior to the short-run calculation. But, as the CEA noted, *such projections must rely on assumptions.*" As we have seen repeatedly, the nuts and bolts of calculations matter. And in this case, the details are not pretty.

There are two serious problems with the $80,000 long-run estimate. The first is obvious: What exactly do we mean by the long run? The 1997 NAS panel chose a 300-year time frame. One does not have to be a big consumer of economic forecasts to know that a 300-year frame is absurd. We can barely predict next year's unemployment rate. How exactly are we supposed to predict the "future path of taxes and government spending as well as economic and demographic trends" for three centuries?

To its credit, the panel also made projections based on more reasonable assumptions. If the long run involved only a 25-year time frame, for example, the $80,000 gain became an $18,000 loss, and if the long run extended over 50 years, the gain fell to $11,000. Not surprisingly, those alternative estimates did not receive media or political attention.

The calculation of the long-run impact must also confront the fact that the current fiscal path of the United States is not sustainable, so much depends on the assumed "future path of taxes and government spending." The 1997 NAS panel solved this issue by making the following assumption:

Starting in 2016, and thereafter, fiscal policy will hold the debt/ GDP ratio constant at the level of 2016.[13]

In plain English, in the year 2016—coincidentally, the year this book is being published—the federal government will either cut benefits substantially or pass a huge tax increase so that the debt problem does not worsen thereafter. As the last line of Table 9.2 shows, if the NAS had not made this assumption, the $80,000 gain would quickly have become a $15,000 loss (even with the 300-year time horizon). In other words, an out-of-the-blue assumption about future taxes and spending built in the conclusion that immigration in the long run is fiscally beneficial because we can spread the pain of paying off our *already accumulated* debt over a larger population. Without this assumption, the taxes paid by the immigrant and descendants would not cover the additional expenditures they would trigger.

This historical account of what the NAS did back in 1997 is educational because we can now see whether the assumption about the future path of taxes and government spending held up. Despite the narrative building and nice sound bites that came out of this computational exercise, the attempt to predict the future turned out to be ludicrously wrong. The often-trumpeted "finding" that immigration generated an $80,000 fiscal benefit per immigrant turned out to be nothing more than arbitrary wishful thinking.

With these lessons in mind, the 2016 NAS panel estimated the long-run fiscal impact today, using a perhaps more realistic 75-year time span for the long run and a wider array of plausible scenarios. The update highlights the importance of two distinct assumptions. First, the estimated impact is again very sensitive to the assumed future path of taxes and spending. Second, the impact changes dramatically if we allow for the possibility that immigrants increase the cost of providing such government services as national defense. As an economist would put it, many government programs are a "public good"; their cost would remain unchanged if we added one more person to our club. For example, the existing military infrastructure can certainly extend its protective shield to *one* additional immigrant without any increase in costs. It is hard to believe, however, that the cost of public goods would be unaffected if we admitted over 40 million immigrants.[*]

Table 9.3 summarizes the bottom line in various scenarios, including the possibility that an immigrant increases the cost of public goods by what it costs to provide that same service to a native and that the United States pursues the "future path of taxes and government spending" used by the Congressional Budget Office (CBO) in its fiscal projections. The average immigrant is fiscally beneficial only if that immigrant does not increase the cost of public goods *and* taxes rise (or benefits are cut) in the future, as projected by the CBO. Oth-

---

TABLE 9.3. LONG-RUN FISCAL IMPACT OF THE AVERAGE IMMIGRANT (2016 NAS REPORT)

	Gain or loss	
	Assuming the future path of taxes and spending stipulated by the CBO	Assuming the current path of taxes and spending continues into the future
Immigrants do not increase the cost of public goods	+$58,000	−$36,000
Immigrants increase the cost of public goods	−$5,000	−$119,000

Source: Francine D. Blau and Christopher Mackie, eds., *The Economic and Fiscal Consequences of Immigration* (Washington, DC): National Academy Press, 2016), Table 8-11.

---

[*] The 1997 NAS report assumed that immigrants did not increase the cost of public goods.

erwise, the $58,000 long-term gain turns into a loss that might be as large as $119,000.*

It may seem preferable to replace arbitrary assumptions about the "future path of taxes and government spending" with more sophisticated expert opinion about what the future will look like, such as the Congressional Budget Office fiscal projections for the next 75 years. Doing so would seem to provide the veneer of a seal of approval by experts in fiscal matters. Nevertheless, it is worth remembering that CBO forecasts are often wrong—*and sometimes they are very wrong even in the very short run.* As an example of the experts' fallibility, consider a news report dated October 19, 2015, about enrollment in ObamaCare insurance programs:

> The Obama administration is having trouble selling insurance plans to healthy people. . . . Last Thursday, the administration predicted enrollment for 2016 will be less than half what the Congressional Budget Office predicted in March.[14]

The CBO's inability to forecast in March 2015 what would happen seven months later is not reassuring. It would not be too cynical to surmise that calculations based on their 75-year fiscal projections of taxes and government spending would be as useful (or useless) as the calculations based on any other set of arbitrary assumption about the fiscal future of the United States.

The fact that different scenarios in Table 9.3 generate both large negative and large positive numbers does not necessarily imply that the "true" effect somehow hovers around zero. The variation instead reflects our ignorance. We simply do not know which scenario is most realistic, how the path of taxes and government spending will evolve

---

* The panel also estimated the fiscal impact separately for immigrants in different education groups. Regardless of the scenario, the admission of a foreign-born high school dropout generates a fiscal loss, and the admission of a college graduate is fiscally beneficial.

over the remainder of this century, and how spending in public goods reacts to large supply shocks.

Let me conclude by reemphasizing the obvious. It is very easy to manipulate the calculations and generate either very large fiscal gains or very large fiscal losses. For example, it is easy to generate a large deficit by charging immigrants for the cost of the public goods they receive. And it is equally easy to generate a large gain by playing around with the assumptions about future taxes and expenditures.

In my view, the sensitivity of the bottom line to this type of tweaking—a tweaking that is extremely tempting in the contentious immigration debate—makes the entire exercise futile, particularly because we have little clue about how immigrants affect the cost of providing public goods and we have no clue about the future path of taxes and government spending.

3. AND IN THE END . . .

THE MOST CREDIBLE estimate of the immigration surplus—the increase in native wealth resulting from immigrant participation in the productive life of our country—is about $50 billion annually. As long as we focus on economic effects, the bottom line that really matters will contrast this surplus with the fiscal impact. If immigration is a boon on the fiscal side, with immigrants paying far more in taxes than they take out, the $50 billion gain will increase, and will increase dramatically, if we can place any trust in some of the long-run estimates. However, if immigration is a net loss fiscally, as is certainly the case with the short-run estimates, the immigration surplus will quickly start dwindling, and the net gain could get dangerously close to zero and perhaps become negative.

If we take the most conservative estimate of the short-run fiscal impact seriously, the fiscal burden essentially offsets the $50 billion surplus, so that immigration barely affects the size of the "economic pie" accruing to natives. In the long term, the estimates of the fiscal impact are far too dependent on arbitrary assumptions to make them a reliable basis for any kind of cost-benefit calculation. The most credible evidence, therefore, suggests that it is not far-fetched to conclude that immigration is a net economic wash.

This conclusion contradicts the narrative that immigration is good for everyone. It also contradicts the claim that immigration is harming the average American. Instead, the reality is much more nuanced. Although the mythical average person may be unaffected, immigration creates many winners and losers. This redistribution of wealth— in an economy where the size of the native economic pie remains relatively fixed—is the key insight I have gleaned from decades of research on the economics of immigration. After all is said and done, immigration turns out to be just another government redistribution program. And this lesson sheds a lot of light on which groups are on which side of the immigration wars.

10

Who Are You Rooting For?

IT IS THE end of the journey and time to ask: What does it all add up to? What lessons have we learned? Can we trust them? And what do they imply about how to proceed?

I have stressed three basic themes throughout the book. And it is useful to keep those themes in mind as we try to think through the implications for any discussion of immigration policy.

First, there are two conflicting perspectives on who the immigrants are, and one of them is just plain wrong. Immigrants are not just labor inputs: robotic workers who move to a new country to fill predetermined slots along the proverbial widget assembly line; whose sole role in life is to produce more widgets; who somehow cleanly and easily disappear from public concern after they step out of the factory gates or once their productive value has been exhausted; and whose presence does not affect the social, political, and cultural fabric of the receiving country.

Immigrants, as Max Frisch wisely remarked, are people. And people make choices. And those choices have many unintended consequences. These real-world human beings choose whether to migrate or not, and those who do move might not be precisely the type that the receiving country was looking for; the migrants choose how to adapt to their new surroundings, and those choices determine whether they and their children assimilate; the migrants live lives outside the factory gates, and there are both gains and losses to be had by what happens out there; and the migrants alter the social and economic infrastructure of the country in countless (and often unpredictable) ways.

Second, the voluminous body of empirical research on the economics of immigration does not give us a simple formula that we can use to predict the impact of future supply shocks. Once we move away from viewing immigrants as robotic workers to viewing them as people, we have to acknowledge that what happens often depends on the political, cultural, social, and economic environment where the migration took place.

Because the factors that define the immigrant experience—the incentive to move, to assimilate, and so on—are specific to time and place, the consequences of a particular supply shock may not be reproducible, and they may provide little information about what would happen in another time or in another place. Even though this insight is universally ignored, it is folly to believe that whatever happened as a result of the immigrants who entered the United States in the early 1900s can be used to predict the impact of Turkish migration to Germany in the 1960s or of mass migration to our country today or of the flood of Syrian refugees entering Europe as I am putting the finishing touches on this book.

Finally, it is wise to be skeptical of expert opinion in politically contentious topics like immigration. The strong influence of the narrative that immigration is "good for everyone" makes it imperative that we carefully examine the nuts and bolts of exactly how we learn certain things about its impact.

Unfortunately, the nuts and bolts are often hidden in obscure technical discussions, making them inaccessible to most nonspecialists. That is why I have repeatedly attempted to clarify the underlying details. A key lesson: the nuts and bolts matter. An assumption here or a data manipulation there makes a difference, and it can often make a big difference in determining the takeaway point. Estimates of the impact of immigration and promises of what will happen are intrinsically tied to the *choice* of conceptual assumptions and statistical manipulations. And we should treat those choices, particularly when there exists a temptation to further an ideological narrative, with all the suspicion they deserve.

Before I turn to the evidence, let me note that I began this book by describing some of the personal circumstances that led, in a very circuitous way, to my professional interest in immigration. My role in the trenches of immigration research raises a couple of paradoxes that many readers might have detected and be curious about. Let me address the first of these puzzles now. As Paul Collier observed, social scientists "have strained every muscle" to build the politically correct narrative that immigration is good for everyone. I never did that type of heavy lifting. Nevertheless, my career somehow progressed nicely.

I was able to get away with this because the issues addressed by the main research papers I wrote on immigration—such as how to measure assimilation or how to measure the labor market impact or how to measure the economic gains for the native population—skirted the ideology that increasingly suffocates the immigration debate. They were how-to papers—technical contributions that addressed very specific questions about how to measure a number of great interest.

Many of the answers implied by my how-to papers did not support the narrative, so they might seem easy to ignore. My solutions are difficult to discount, however, because they are the solutions that follow easily from the theory and statistical methods that are widely used in mainstream economics. For better or worse, little in my research departs from the standard ways in which economists think about and measure outcomes in the labor market.

It has been three decades since I began to think about immigration seriously. What do I take away from the evidence? Which insights do I find most useful when the time comes to think about the future of immigration policy?

- Not everyone wants to move to the United States, and those who choose to move are fundamentally different from those who choose to stay behind. The nature of the selection, however, can vary dramatically from place to place. The United States will attract high-skill workers when we offer a higher payoff for their abilities, but the high-skill workers will stay behind if they can get a better deal at home. The fact that different kinds of people will want to move out of different countries (and that the skills they bring are not always transferable to the American setting) creates considerable inequality in economic outcomes across immigrant groups at the time of their arrival.

- Assimilation is not inevitable. The speed of economic assimilation—the narrowing of the gap in economic outcomes between immigrants and natives—depends crucially on conditions on the ground. Sometimes those conditions speed up the process, and sometimes they slow it down. In fact, economic assimilation today is far slower than it was two or three decades ago. This trend, however, masks crucial differences in the assimilation of different immigrant groups. Some groups assimilate very rapidly and some do not. Typically, groups that are more skilled and that do not have access to large and vibrant ethnic enclaves assimilate faster.

- The experience of the descendants of the Ellis Island–era immigrants shows that the melting pot did indeed melt away the differences in economic outcomes across those ethnic groups, but it took nearly a century for the melting pot to do its job. The same process may be starting to take place with the current mass migration, as the children of today's immigrants earn higher wages and exhibit less ethnic inequality than their parents did. But we truly do not know how things will pan out in the next few decades, because the economic and social conditions that kept the melting pot busy throughout the 1900s may not be reproducible in the next century.

- Immigrants affect the job opportunities of natives. The laws of supply and demand apply to the price of labor just as much as to the price of gas. The data suggest that a 10 percent increase in the number of workers in a particular skill group probably lowers the wage of that group by at least 3 percent. The temptation to play with assumptions and manipulate the data, however, is particularly strong when examining this very contentious issue, so the reported effects often depend on such assumptions and manipulations. Our look inside the black box of how research is done suggests one lesson: the more one aggregates skill groups, the more likely one hides away the specific group of affected workers—making it harder to document whether immigration made anyone worse off. The more laser-focused the group of native workers examined, the easier it is to detect that immigration affected the targeted group.

- Immigrant participation in the workforce redistributes wealth from those who compete with immigrants to those who use immigrants. But because the gains accruing to the winners exceed the losses suffered by the losers, immigrants create an "immigration surplus," a net increase in the aggregate wealth of the native population. However, the surplus is small, about $50 billion annually. That calculation *also* suggests a half-trillion-dollar redistribution of wealth from workers to firms. The surplus could be much larger, if there are many exceptional immigrants and if some of the unique abilities brought by those immigrants rub off on the native workforce.

- The welfare state introduces the possibility that the gains measured by the immigration surplus might disappear if immigrants are net users of social assistance programs rather than net contributors. There is little doubt that immigrants receive assistance at higher rates than natives, creating a fiscal burden in the short run. In the long run, immigration may be fiscally beneficial because the unfunded liabilities in Social Security and Medicare are unsustainable and will require either a substantial increase in taxes or a substantial cut in benefits. Immigrants expand the taxpayer base, perhaps helping to spread out the burden. It is extremely difficult to accurately measure the fiscal benefit in the long run, however, because much depends on the assumptions made about the future path of taxes and government spending.

- It is probably not too far-fetched to conclude that, at least in the short run, the economic gains captured by the immigration surplus are offset by the fiscal burden of providing public services to immigrants. Given the scale and the skill mix of the immigrants who entered our country in the past few decades, the economic impact of immigration, *on average*, is at best a wash. This near-zero effect conceals a substantial redistribution of wealth from workers to firms.

- The argument that open borders would exponentially increase the economic gains from immigration depends crucially on the perspective of immigrants as workers rather than immigrants as people. The multi-trillion-dollar gains promised by the proponents of open borders could quickly disappear (and even become an economic debacle) if immigrants adversely influence the social, political, and economic fabric of receiving countries. In the end, the impact of open borders will depend not only on whether the movers bring along their raw labor and productive skills, but also on whether they bring the institutional, cultural, and political baggage that may have hampered development in the poor countries.

Social scientists in general, and economists in particular, have done a very good job of convincing many people that the mathematical models we build and the empirical findings we generate can be the foundation for a "scientific" determination of social policy. Put differently, if all the expert modeling and statistical analysis says that the world looks like *x*, then policy *y* must be the right thing to do. The fact that the social science research community was able to convince the rest of the world that our work had this type of intrinsic value certainly increased the demand for our services, raised our incomes, got us invited on many nice junkets, and made us feel that our efforts were being appreciated and rewarded.

Ironically, I have been employed by the Harvard Kennedy School for the past two decades, probably the premier place to study public policy in the world. Nevertheless, I happen to believe that the claim that mathematical modeling and data analysis can somehow lead to a scientific determination of social policy is sheer nonsense. Social policy could not be scientifically determined *even if* there were universal agreement on the underlying facts. Ideology and values matter as well. And openly acknowledging that obvious reality, instead of peddling particular policy goals as if they were implied by some scientific study, would make the debate over politically contentious issues such as immigration far more honest and productive.

The argument that models and data can somehow lead to a purely technocratic determination of public policy ignores a simple fact of life: politicians often pursue a particular policy goal because they— and the people who elected them—believe that what they are doing is *the right thing to do*.

We all have different values and perceptions about what is right, many of them coming from our personal history and from the ideological compass that we use to navigate through life. Some of us feel that we should have more immigration because of the diversity that immigrants introduce into our culture; some people will go much further and argue that it is immoral to deny any person the right to cross a national boundary in search of a better life. On the other side, some people want to change the types of immigrants we admit, arguing that one type is better in some sense than another type. And still others believe that we need to substantially cut immigration because they want to preserve particular things about the country as it is now.

Often, from each side's perspective, the other side's arguments make little sense and are dismissed as being misguided, factually incorrect, or immoral. But that is what the political process is for. We will not all agree on what we, as a country, should do about immigration, but "we the people" will vote and elect representatives who will, presumably, pursue the objectives that got them elected.

Suppose, for example, that a democratically elected government runs on a platform promising to reduce world poverty by increasing foreign aid *and* by allowing many of the world's poor to move to the United States to partake in the many opportunities that our country offers. The politicians consult the experts on a nice junket in Maui, and all the experts agree about the fiscal impact. Of course, the notion that the science is settled is as far-fetched an assumption as one can make in a politically contentious research area, but it helps to illustrate the point nicely. In particular, let's assume that low-skill immigration is, in fact, a fiscal burden.

Does learning that the poor and huddled masses create a fiscal burden deter the democratically elected government from carrying out its mandate? The answer likely depends on the "burden threshold" that the government and its supporters are willing to accept. If the burden per native household was only a few hundred dollars per year, the politically sensible policy would be to admit millions of low-skill immigrants. After all, the government promised to reduce world poverty, and to spend a lot of money to do so. Although there might be second thoughts if the fiscal burden was in the tens of thousands of dollars, ideology would clearly trump facts for a large range of the fiscal burden. This burden is the price that the people who are ideologically committed to the reduction in world poverty are willing to pay for doing good. In the end, the policy adopted has little to do with the underlying facts, and much to do with the motivating ideology.

The modeling and statistical work that the experts perform are still useful, but only in a limited sense. The expert can multiply the fiscal burden resulting from a low-skill immigrant by the number of such immigrants admitted. Put differently, the modeling and the statistics tell us the cost of pursuing a particular political goal, a goal that may not be financially beneficial but that somehow makes at least some of us better off in intangible ways. In the end, different beliefs about the right thing to do will often lead to different immigration policies, regardless of what the underlying models and data say.

Choosing among alternative policies becomes even more difficult when the gains and losses are not evenly distributed. It is easy to imagine, within the context of the fiscal burden example I just contrived, that some native households will pay a greater share of the costs of low-skill immigration. The distribution of the "pain" might depend on income (progressive income taxation would imply that the fiscal burden is more heavily borne by wealthier households) or on where the natives live (some of the assistance is funded by local and state governments).

In some utopian world, a proposed new social policy would be a win-win situation. That new law or regulation would increase *everyone's* well-being, and we would all quickly sign on to the plan and go along with the proposed change.

Unfortunately, as much as we might prefer to think otherwise, any proposed policy change is typically not good for everyone. Despite all the wishful thinking and the dominant narrative, immigration does create winners and losers. The adoption of *any* immigration policy implicitly makes a statement not only about how much we care about immigrants as compared to natives, but also about how much we care about *this* particular group of natives versus *that* particular group of natives.

Let me state this point as clearly as I can. In the end, the choice of an immigration policy is driven by the answer to: *Who are you rooting for?* The mathematical models and the statistical manipulations might put a veneer of science on the policy proposals, but the policy choice is driven mainly by our ideological conviction that one group should benefit at the expense of another.

One particular objective that some people might find attractive is the idea that immigration should generate the largest possible immigration surplus (net of whatever fiscal burden there might be). In other words, we should pursue a policy that makes natives wealthy. This goal has certainly played a role in the debate throughout US history. Economic arguments that prove or disprove some perceived cost or benefit for the native population are tossed around very often.

If our goal is indeed to make natives as rich as possible, the accumulated knowledge from economic research tells us exactly how to get there: we should admit only high-skill immigrants. High-skill immigrants are most complementary with the productive resources we already have. *And* if many of the high-skill immigrants had exceptional talents, the increase in the immigration surplus would be much larger because we could all become much more productive. *And* we would not need to worry about the fiscal burden; high-skill immigrants would share the cost of the welfare state and help pay for all the liabilities that will have to be funded as we grow old. *Plus*, as icing on the cake, high-skill immigration would help us achieve a more egalitarian society in the long run: low-skill natives would not see their wages reduced, and high-skill natives would face more labor market competition.

But this policy goal, like any other policy goal, is based on a particular set of values: the notion that making the "economic pie" accruing to the native population as big as possible is the right thing to do. This type of goal is certainly ingrained in the way that many economists think. The pursuit of "efficiency," of adopting policies that maximize some notion of aggregate wealth, becomes almost second nature after a few years of training in economics. I suspect, however, that many people would have difficulty buying into the notion that this is what immigration *should* accomplish. And despite my own economics background, I, too, have increasingly felt that the single-minded pursuit of efficiency does not necessarily produce the kind of world that I would like to live in.

It is not hard to imagine that in a representative democracy where only natives vote, the elected politicians would have already enacted this particular immigration policy *if that is what the majority of voters truly wanted.* It is obvious, however, that this is not the policy we have chosen to pursue. For whatever reason, the policy we do pursue brings in both low-skill immigrants (legally and illegally) and high-skill immigrants.

There is little doubt that the United States could benefit much more—*in economic terms*—by shifting away from this mixed-skills policy to one that reduced the number of the poor and huddled masses and instead admitted more high-skill immigrants. The fact that we have repeatedly chosen not to make such a change is informative, and that "revealed preference" should not be ignored.

Perhaps, in the grand scheme of things, the mixed-skills policy makes some sense. It may reflect a compromise between two polar views of what immigration should be about. It gives many of the world's poor a chance to improve their lot in life, and many people would think of that outcome as ultimately a good thing. At the same time, the mixed-skills policy allows for the entry of many high-skill immigrants, the immigrants who generate most of the economic gains and help pay the bill. In short, the policy that we actually pursue allows the country both to do good and to collect at least some financial returns at the same time.

The problem with the mixed-skills policy is not that it leaves some potential economic gains on the table; "we the people" have repeatedly chosen to forgo those gains. The problem lies with the fact that it does not address the economic dislocations or fiscal consequences created by the entry of large numbers of workers in specific skill groups or occupations. In other words, the problem with our current immigration policy is that the gains and losses are not equitably shared by the American people. If we were to take the calculation of the immigration surplus seriously, the transfer from the losers to the winners would be on the order of a half-trillion dollars.

Just like the auto workers in Detroit back in the 1970s, who bore the brunt of the impact of globalization through international trade, low-educated native workers know full well that current immigration does not benefit them. And if we are going to pursue a policy that gives the huddled masses a chance at the American dream, we are also going to have to think of ways to somehow protect those disadvantaged natives, including many vulnerable minorities, from the economic dislocations that low-skill immigration inevitably unleashes.

It is not only the workers at the bottom of the distribution that lose out from the mixed-skills policy. High-skill immigration also imposes costs, and those costs are borne by very specific groups, such as the computer programmers competing against H-1B visa holders or American mathematicians affected by the influx of Soviet mathematicians. The possibility that the presence of skilled foreigners in these very narrow fields might increase the potential for future innovation does little to address the current grievance of the natives who have been displaced and who may no longer be able to pursue the careers they were trained for.

It would be easy to bury one's head in the sand and simply claim that we could avoid some of these problems—such as the fiscal burden from low-skill immigration—by building a wall around the welfare state. The fact is that no such wall has been built, and it is unlikely that we will build one in the foreseeable future. Low-skill immigration does create a fiscal burden, and the high rates of welfare use by low-skill immigrants may create future problems. But these problems remain unaddressed if we simply daydream that in an ideal world we could build a wall and prevent immigrants from entering the garden of public benefits.

Another way of burying one's head in the sand is to endlessly repeat the mantra "immigration is good for everyone" until everyone is indeed convinced that immigration is like manna from heaven. But wishing something to be true, and building a narrative designed to convince many people that the wish has come true, does not, in fact, make it true. Let me ask a very simple question: Would we even be bothering to debate immigration if everybody in the United States had actually become much wealthier after we welcomed over 40 million immigrants?

The politically correct narrative is wrong: immigration is *not* good for everyone. And we would do a much better job of figuring out what to do if we could drop the pretense that everybody is better off and instead try to address the problems created by the fact that there are both winners and losers.

A more constructive approach would be to admit outright that the pursuit of any specific immigration policy has little to do with facts, and much to do with ideology and values. Who are *you* rooting for?

A more constructive approach would be to precisely identify the winners and the losers resulting from the mixed-skills policy that we now pursue (or any other policy we might pursue in the future). By identifying who wins and who loses, we could then perhaps think of ways in which some of the losses could be prevented and some of the gains could be more equitably distributed.

A more constructive approach would openly recognize the obvious contradiction between pushing for large-scale low-skill immigration and the presence of a welfare state. Wishful thinking about a world without welfare will not do. The welfare state is here to stay, and we need to somehow balance the desire to do good by admitting the huddled masses with the incentives that the welfare state creates. It is not only a problem of the dollars and cents involved, but also that the welfare state might affect the long-term economic, political, and social integration of the immigrant family.

A more constructive approach would keep in mind the distinction between immigrants as workers and immigrants as people. Large-scale movements of people will have many unintended consequences, and there is much we do not know about those consequences. If nothing else, being aware of this crucial distinction should lessen the temptation to advocate huge and sudden increases in immigration, such as the zeal behind the open-border movement that would radically rearrange the world order, or the rush to enact thousand-page statutes that few read, that even fewer understand, and that offer the false panacea of "comprehensive immigration reform." In short, prudence and caution are traits that would serve us well in the immigration context.

Let me now address the second paradox that many readers might have detected. I am an immigrant, and I benefited immensely from the opportunity to live my life in this exceptional country. Yet I do not buy into the notion that immigration is universally beneficial. Unfortunately, immigration is one of those contentious issues where anyone who enters the arena is quickly pigeonholed into being one of the good guys or the bad guys, where "good" and "bad" depend entirely on one's perspective. The fact that my work has emphasized both the benefits *and* the costs has inevitably led to claims that I am an "immigration skeptic" or simply anti-immigration. And I suspect some people feel that I am the type of immigrant who wanted to close the gates the minute I disembarked from the Pan Am plane that brought me to Miami in 1962.

These reactions have always distressed me because nothing could be further from the truth. Over the years, I have learned that the surest way to ruin a good night's sleep is to read some of the commentaries that mention my work. Whenever I got involved in policy discussions, I tried to be careful and emphasize that such and such a proposal would be best *only if* all we cared about was some type of economic gain. For example, if all we want to do is make natives richer, there is little rationale for admitting low-skill immigrants.

Does that mean I believe that immigration policy should be guided by economic gains alone? Not at all. Does that mean I believe that we should not admit any low-skill immigrants? Most definitely not!

The United States has played a unique and historic role by offering hope and a new life to the many people abroad who have so few choices, and *that* is the kind of country I want to live in. Such a policy is problematic in many ways, creating economic and social dislocations that often target the most disadvantaged Americans. But I still feel that it is a good thing to give some of the poor and huddled masses, people who face so many hardships, a chance to experience the incredible opportunities that our country has to offer. It is a real tragedy that cold-blooded political calculations allowed low-skill immigration to become a political, economic, and logistical mess because of the reluctance to secure our borders. It is an even greater tragedy that we have given no thought to formulating an immigration policy that *responsibly* gives some of the less fortunate a chance at the American dream while simultaneously addressing the problems and dislocations that this type of immigration creates.

I have now described what we can learn from the existing research and the personal baggage I carry when I think about immigration. Some might also be curious to know what I would do about immigration policy *today*.

My answer, of course, depends on what I believe the objective of immigration policy to be. I take it as a given that we will continue to pursue a mixed-skills policy, a policy that generates economic gains by admitting high-skill immigrants but that also "does good" by admitting some of the huddled masses. Within that context, there are indeed some policy shifts that would lead to preferable outcomes. But I do not have all the answers. Some remaining issues are very problematic and do not lend themselves to an easy fix.

Let me start with the obvious. It makes no sense to talk about changes in policy unless our borders are secure. The very porous borders that have allowed over 11 million undocumented persons to enter the United States make legal immigration policy, in Woody Allen's words, "a travesty of a mockery of a sham."[1] What is the point of coming up with ways to improve immigration policy if anyone can become an immigrant by crossing the southern border or by breaking the terms of a tourist visa? A necessary first step is simply to regain control of the border so that changes in immigration policy mean something once again.

A secure border would require vast and ongoing expenditures, and we already spend a lot of money with less-than-stellar results. The undocumented flow might slow down dramatically if we took a different tack: seriously penalizing lawbreaking employers. Holding employers accountable would require them to use an already available electronic system where they could easily check the visa status of job applicants. Fortunately, we are not the type of country that tramples on the civil rights of undocumented immigrants when they are detected and apprehended. But we are certainly the type of country that heavily fines and penalizes those firms that break the law. Sizable fines and criminal penalties would go a long way toward making undocumented immigration a more manageable problem, and such measures would free us to discuss immigration policy in a more sensible and rational way.

I have long felt that the obsession over legislation that grants amnesty to millions of undocumented immigrants is itself a travesty— a "play" performed mainly for political gain by the parties involved. Everyone knows that many, if not most, of the undocumented immigrants could eventually use the family preference system to qualify for legal status under existing laws. Amazingly enough, sometimes inaction is the best action. And benign neglect of this sensitive issue is probably best *as long as* we take concurrent steps to ensure that we need not revisit this problem in the future with an even larger undocumented population. Perhaps in the years ahead, after the incoming flow of undocumented persons has been greatly reduced, it will be politically feasible to speed up the process of granting family visas to much of the current undocumented population.

We also need to view immigration policy from a broader perspective—worrying not only about how many immigrants to accept and what formula to use to select the lucky few, but also about how to alleviate the adverse impact of immigration on many Americans. The best policy response to the lower wages caused by immigration is not necessarily to cut immigration altogether. As we have seen, immigration creates economic benefits. However, the answer to lower wages should not be just to ignore them or to maintain the charade that immigration is good for everyone. The Trade Adjustment Assistance program enacted in 1974 provided aid to workers affected by imports. Perhaps it is time to set up a comparable program to assist the workers employed in industries and localities that are targeted by immigrants.

Many agricultural and service companies have benefited handsomely from the employment of low-skill immigrants, and it is about time we used those excess profits to compensate low-skill Americans for their losses and to help them make the transition to new jobs and occupations. Similarly, let's take the Bill Gates claim at face value: if Microsoft really creates four new jobs for every H-1B visa granted, then Microsoft is profiting substantially from that program and should be willing to pay *many* thousands of dollars for each of those coveted visas. Those funds could be used to compensate and retrain the affected natives in the high-tech industry. We might be pleasantly surprised by how much money firms are willing to pony up to import guest workers. In Singapore, for example, firms that bring in low-skill service workers pay a *monthly* levy of 20–30 percent of the worker's salary for the temporary visa. Put simply, immigration policy should begin to incorporate specific taxes and subsidies to ensure that the gains from immigration are more evenly distributed.

But I am not naïve. To even partially compensate the losers of current policy, massive immigration will require massive new government programs to supervise a massive wealth redistribution totaling tens of billions of dollars. The firms that profit from the way things are would not go along with these transfers without an epic political struggle. And many of those who advocate for more immigration would surely balk at the implied expansion of government. Perhaps *then* we could have a real debate over immigration policy.

Ironically, those are the "easy" fixes. Some of the remaining problems with current immigration policy are even harder to address, at least within the context of what I think immigration should be about.

The link between immigration and the welfare state introduces particularly thorny issues. It *is* worrisome that, despite all the restrictions on welfare use by immigrants, nearly half of immigrant-headed households receive some type of aid. The easiest fix is to do what Australia and Canada do: change the admission rules to select only high-skill applicants. But I truly buy into the exceptional role that our country has played by offering hope to the poor abroad. One solution might then be to further tighten the welfare eligibility rules for immigrants. However, this approach creates additional problems because immigrant households often qualify for assistance by virtue of having US-born children, and effective eligibility restrictions may well require that we treat minor US citizens differently depending on where their parents were born.

An equally difficult problem concerns the long-term assimilation prospects of immigrant families. Historically, immigrants made the decision to assimilate without much government encouragement. This hands-off approach worked well in the past, when the assimilation decision was made in a cultural and social environment where the phrase "melting pot" was not considered to be a microaggression. The current ideological revulsion in many quarters toward the very notion of assimilation, and the continued reinforcement of distinct ethnic identities by many government programs, makes the hands-off approach problematic.

We need only look at the European situation to realize that the presence of large groups of unassimilated minorities sets off many alarms. At the very least, we should revisit the government's role in the assimilation process. Put bluntly, "we the people" need to decide whether the multicultural utopia that progressive ideology peddles makes any sense in the current environment, and whether the many government programs that continually divide us along ethnic lines can coexist with large foreign-born populations.

Finally, the debate over the flood of refugees unleashed by a series of military debacles in the Middle East shows the increasing ambiguity in pursuing the objective of doing good. My own background makes me very sympathetic to the plight of the refugees because they are fleeing intolerable conditions. But we also need to be realists; a few of those refugees bring grudges and conflicts they wish to rekindle, and a few others import cultural attitudes that may undermine the social and political stability of the receiving countries. These spillovers could well determine the long-term impact of such migration. Inevitably, immigration policy will increasingly reflect the notion that immigrants, whether refugees or not, are people who bring with them far more than their raw labor.

Thinking about immigration policy introduces difficult and inescapable trade-offs, and those trade-offs cannot be evaluated solely on the basis of the mathematical modeling and statistical analysis provided by experts. In the end, the policy choice depends mostly on our values, on what we believe the United States is all about, and on what kind of country we want our children to live in.

The overreliance on economic modeling and statistical findings is often a crutch used by those who would rather not reveal their own ideological preferences, but instead cherry-pick among the many conflicting claims in the research studies to promote a policy goal that, deep down, was ideologically predetermined. It would be refreshing if we could reconfigure the immigration debate into a discussion of who we are and how we can ensure that the costs and benefits are more equitably distributed, rather than an argument over how much immigration affects wages or how many dollars the fiscal burden amounts to. The immigration debate is about much more than numbers.

Acknowledgments

I KNOW THE exact moment when the idea for this book was born. Jack Repcheck, an editor at W. W. Norton, was sitting in my office at Harvard on March 30, 2011. I had known Jack for about two decades, had interacted with him when he worked at Princeton University Press, and had connected with him periodically through the years. That day, however, he was passing through Cambridge and stopped by to chat about our mutual interests.

At the time, I was working on a technical book, *Immigration Economics*, which Harvard University Press eventually published. I told Jack that the book laid out a conceptual framework to help inform the professional study of immigration in the future. He agreed that writing such a book was a valuable use of my time, but he also said that what was really needed was a book on immigration that would clarify the debate for the typical reader. I told him that the contentiousness of the immigration debate—and particularly the viciousness of the attacks and counterattacks—had quenched my thirst for being too involved in the public discussion, which is why I had chosen to devote several years of my life to the technical project I had described. Jack insisted that a "short, simple, and direct" book on immigration would have a highly beneficial impact on the policy debate, and he encouraged me to think about it.

The seed that Jack planted in my mind kept growing for quite some time. And soon after *Immigration Economics* was published in June

2014, I e-mailed Jack and told him I was ready. Jack and I met again in Cambridge and, over a very productive lunch, we plotted the organization and approach that this book would take. Tragically, Jack Repcheck passed away unexpectedly in October 2015, shortly after he had read and edited the second draft. The published book, I am glad to say, closely follows the plan that Jack and I outlined at that lunch and incorporates all of Jack's valuable comments and reactions.

Jack, like me, was a lifelong Beatles fan, and he got a big kick out of the Beatles references in one of the chapters. In his life outside Norton, in fact, Jack played guitar in a rock band and performed Beatles classics. I told Jack that the next time he came through Boston, he had to stop by my house to see my collection of Beatles records and memorabilia (a hobby that stopped abruptly the minute I had children). Jack's reaction speaks volumes about the enthusiasm he brought to his work and his music: "I *very* much want to see your collection sometime! We'll celebrate the publication of the book together and maybe you can show me then." Unfortunately, that visit never came to pass, but I know that Jack would have had a splendid time perusing the material. I truly hope that Jack would have been proud of how this book turned out.

I was very fortunate that John Glusman took over editing duties prior to preparation of the final draft. John's able editing streamlined the manuscript in important ways and helped focus key parts of the book. I am also grateful to Alexa Pugh at Norton, who patiently answered many questions that helped ease the manuscript's transition from a computer file to a printed volume.

Many colleagues, friends, and acquaintances, far too numerous to mention individually, have read many drafts of my work over the years, as well as early drafts of this book. They know that I have always been grateful for their input and assistance, and that even the most critical remarks have been useful because they have forced me to rethink what I am trying to accomplish. The same goes for the many coauthors (about fifteen, and counting!) that I have been fortunate to work with in my immigration research. Each of them has affected how I think about things, and I know that they will be able to detect the influence of our collaboration.

Finally, my greatest debt is to my family. A big chunk of the years I devoted to studying immigration happily coincided with the period during which my wife and I raised our children, Sarah, Timothy, and Rebecca. I was truly fortunate to have been able to see my kids grow into caring and responsible young adults. And I am forever indebted to my wife, Jane. I would never have been able to reach the point of being able to write this book without her patience, her cooperation, and her love.

Lexington, Massachusetts
December 11, 2015

Notes

Chapter 1.

1. Paul Collier, *Exodus: How Migration Is Changing Our World* (New York: Oxford University Press, 2013), 25–26; emphasis added.
2. The paper was published in 1978; see Barry R. Chiswick, "The Effect of Americanization on the Earnings of Foreign-Born Men," *Journal of Political Economy* 86 (1978).
3. There are indeed sizable skill differences across the different waves of Cuban immigrants; see Madeline Zavodny, "Race, Wages, and Assimilation among Cuban Immigrants," *Population Research and Policy Review* 21 (2003).
4. George J. Borjas, *Friends or Strangers: The Impact of Immigrants on the U.S. Economy* (New York: Basic Books, 1990).
5. Julian Simon, *The Economic Consequences of Immigration* (Cambridge, MA: Blackwell, 1989).
6. Borjas, *Friends or Strangers*, 81.

Chapter 2.

1. Joseph E. Stiglitz, "The Broken Promise of NAFTA," *New York Times*, January 6, 2004.
2. Louis Uchitelle, "NAFTA Should Have Stopped Illegal Immigration, Right?" *New York Times*, February 18, 2007.
3. Bob Hamilton and John Whalley, "Efficiency and Distributional Implications of Global Restrictions on Labour Mobility: Calculations and Policy Implications," *Journal of Development Economics* 14 (1984).
4. Alex Tabarrok, "The Case for Getting Rid of Borders—Completely," *Atlantic*, October 10, 2015.
5. Michael A. Clemens, "Economics and Emigration: Trillion-Dollar Bills on the Sidewalk?" *Journal of Economic Perspectives* 25 (2011).
6. "In Praise of Huddled Masses," *Wall Street Journal*, July 3, 1984.
7. Michael A. Clemens, Claudio E. Montenegro, and Lant Pritchett, "The Place Premium: Wage Differences for Identical Workers across the U.S. Border," Center for Global Development Working Paper no. 148, 2008.

8. Daron Acemoglu and James Robinson, *Why Nations Fail: The Origins of Power, Prosperity, and Poverty* (New York: Crown, 2012).

9. Paul Collier, *Exodus: How Migration Is Changing Our World* (New York: Oxford University Press, 2013), 33, 34.

10. Ibid., 68.

11. Raymond Fisman and Edward Miguel, "Corruption, Norms, and Legal Enforcement: Evidence from Diplomatic Parking Tickets," *Journal of Political Economy* 115 (2007).

12. Robert D. Putnam, *Bowling Alone: The Collapse and Revival of American Community* (New York: Simon and Schuster, 2000).

13. Robert D. Putnam, "E Pluribus Unum: Diversity and Community in the Twenty-First Century—The 2006 Johan Skytte Prize Lecture," *Scandinavian Political Studies* 30 (2007): 137.

14. Ibid., 165.

Chapter 3.

1. Richard Easterlin, "Immigration: Economic and Social Characteristics," in *Harvard Encyclopedia of American Ethnic Groups*, eds. Stephan Thernstrom, Ann Orlov, and Oscar Handlin (Cambridge, MA: Harvard University Press, 1980), 476.

2. *Yuen Sang Low v. Attorney General*, 479 F.2nd 820 (9th Cir. 1973).

3. *Drax v. Reno*, 338 F.3rd 98, 99–100 (2nd Cir. 2003).

4. Edward P. Hutchinson, *Legislative History of American Immigration Policy, 1798–1965* (Philadelphia: University of Pennsylvania Press, 1981), 391.

5. Francis A. Walker, "Restriction of Immigration," *Atlantic Monthly*, June 1896.

6. David M. Reimers, *Still the Golden Door: The Third World Comes to America* (New York: Columbia University Press, 1992), 74.

7. Elliott Abrams and Franklin S. Abrams, "Immigration Policy—Who Gets In and Why," *Public Interest* 38 (1975), 8.

8. "UFW History," United Farm Workers, http://www.ufw.org, accessed December 1, 2015.

9. Myrna Garcia, "Immigration Reform and Control Act," in *Undocumented Immigrants in the United States: An Encyclopedia of Their Experience*, ed. Anna Ochoa O'Leary (Westport, CT: Greenwood, 2014), 383.

10. Gordon H. Hanson, "The Economic Logic of Illegal Immigration," Council of Foreign Relations, Council Special Report no. 26, April 2007, 14–16.

11. Bryan Baker and Nancy Rytina, "Estimates of the Unauthorized Immigrant Population Residing in the United States: January 2012," US Department of Homeland Security, March 2013.

12. "Estimates of the Unauthorized Immigrant Population Residing in the United States: 1990 to 2000," US Immigration and Naturalization Service, 2003, 3.

13. Jeremy B. White, "Driver's License Demand Surges," *Sacramento Bee*, April 3, 2015.

Chapter 4.

1. Quoted in Dale Hanson Bourke, *Immigration: Tough Questions, Direct Answers* (Downers Grove, IL: Intervarsity Press, 2014), 106.
2. Edmund S. Morgan, ed., *Not Your Usual Founding Father: Selected Readings from Benjamin Franklin* (New Haven, CT: Yale University Press, 2006), 162.
3. Roger Ebert, "El Norte," rogerebert.com, August 1, 2004; "RNC 2012: Mitt Romney Acceptance Speech to GOP Convention," *Washington Post*, August 30, 2012; Dave Boyer, "Obama Welcomes New U.S. Citizens, Vows to Fix 'Broken' Immigration System," *Washington Times*, July 4, 2014.
4. Leslie Colitt, "Escape from East Berlin," *Guardian*, August 16, 2011.
5. Central Intelligence Agency, Office of Current Intelligence, "The East German Refugees" (memo, August 10, 1961); emphasis added.
6. Erhan Artuc, Shubham Chaudhuri, and John McLaren, "Trade Shocks and Labor Adjustment: A Structural Empirical Approach," *American Economic Review* 100 (2010); Simone Bertoli, Jesús Fernández-Huertas Moraga, and Francesc Ortega, "Crossing the Border: Self-Selection, Earnings, and Individual Migration Decisions," *Journal of Development Economics* 101 (2013).
7. Darren Lubotsky, "The Effect of Changes in the U.S. Wage Structure on Recent Immigrants' Earnings," *Review of Economics and Statistics* 93 (2011).
8. James P. Smith and Barry Edmonston, eds., *The New Americans: Economic, Demographic, and Fiscal Effects of Immigration* (Washington, DC: National Academy Press, 1997), 190.
9. George J. Borjas, "Self-Selection and the Earnings of Immigrants," *American Economic Review* 77 (1987).
10. Paula Stephan, *How Economics Shapes Science* (Cambridge, MA: Harvard University Press, 2012), 165.
11. Ibid., 176.
12. National Research Council, *Trends in the Early Careers of Life Scientists* (Washington, DC: National Academy Press, 1998), 5.
13. "Donald Trump Announces a Presidential Bid," *Washington Post*, June 16, 2015.
14. Daniel Chiquiar and Gordon H. Hanson, "International Migration, Self-Selection, and the Distribution of Wages: Evidence from Mexico and the United States," *Journal of Political Economy* 113 (2005).
15. Jesús Fernández-Huertas Moraga, "New Evidence on Emigrant Selection," *Review of Economics and Statistics* 93 (2011); Robert Kaestner and Ofer Malamud, "Self-Selection and International Migration: New Evidence from Mexico," *Review of Economics and Statistics* 96 (2014).
16. David Lagakos et al., "Life-Cycle Human Capital Accumulation across

Countries: Lessons from U.S. Immigrants," National Bureau of Economic Research Working Paper no. 21914, January 2016.

17. Sherrie A. Kossoudji and Deborah A. Cobb-Clark, "Coming Out of the Shadows: Learning about Legal Status and Wages from the Legalized Population," *Journal of Labor Economics* 20 (2002); Neeraj Kaushal, "Amnesty Programs and the Labor Market Outcomes of Undocumented Workers," *Journal of Human Resources* 16 (2006).

18. "The Economic Status of Asian Americans and Pacific Islanders in the Wake of the Great Recession" (US Department of Labor, 2014), 9.

19. Stephen J. Trejo, "Why Do Mexican Americans Earn Low Wages?" *Journal of Political Economy* 105 (1997): 1235.

Chapter 5.

1. Yann Algan et al., "The Economic Situation of First and Second-Generation Immigrants in France, Germany and the United Kingdom," *Economic Journal* 120 (2010): F4–F5.

2. Samuel Huntington, "The Hispanic Challenge," *Foreign Policy*, March/April 2004, 36; see also Samuel Huntington, *Who Are We? The Challenges to American National Identity* (New York: Simon and Schuster, 2004).

3. Huntington, "Hispanic Challenge," 43.

4. David Brooks, "The Americano Dream," *New York Times*, February 24, 2004.

5. Jacob Vigdor, "Measuring Immigrant Assimilation in the United States," Civic Report no. 53 (Center for Civic Innovation at the Manhattan Institute, May 2008).

6. Dowell Myers and John Pitkin, "Assimilation Today: New Evidence Shows the Latest Immigrants to America Are Following in Our History's Footsteps" (Center for American Progress, September 2010), 30.

7. Arnold Schwarzenegger, *Total Recall: My Unbelievably True Life Story* (New York: Simon and Schuster, 2013), 137–38; emphasis added.

8. Jose Antonio Vargas, "My Life as an Undocumented Immigrant," *New York Times Magazine*, June 22, 2011.

9. "America's Assimilating Hispanics," *Wall Street Journal*, June 18, 2013.

10. George J. Borjas, "Assimilation, Changes in Cohort Quality, and the Earnings of Immigrants," *Journal of Labor Economics* 3 (1985).

11. The assimilation rate would decline if the data were adjusted for return migration; see Darren Lubotsky, "Chutes or Ladders? A Longitudinal Analysis of Immigrant Earnings," *Journal of Political Economy* 115 (2007).

12. Darren Lubotsky, "The Effect of Changes in the U.S. Wage Structure on Recent Immigrants' Earnings," *Review of Economics and Statistics* 93 (2011).

13. Adrianna Oudman, "Young and Undocumented," *Banner*, January 18, 2011.

14. Timothy Hatton, "The Immigrant Assimilation Puzzle in Late Nineteenth-Century America," *Journal of Economic History* 57 (1997).

15. Ran Abramitzky, Leah Platt Boustan, and Katherine Eriksson, "A Nation

of Immigrants: Assimilation and Economic Outcomes in the Age of Mass Migration," *Journal of Political Economy* 122 (2014): 469–70.

16. Edward P. Lazear, "Culture and Language," *Journal of Political Economy* 107 (1999): S95.

17. Alejandro Portes and Robert D. Manning, "The Immigrant Enclave: Theory and Empirical Examples," in *Competitive Ethnic Relations*, eds. Joan Nagel and Susan Olzak (Orlando, FL: Academic Press, 1986), 63–64.

18. Jimy Sanders and Victor Nee, "Limits of Ethnic Solidarity in the Enclave Economy," *American Sociological Review* 52 (1987): 762.

19. Jacob Vigdor, "New York City and the Genius of Immigrant Assimilation," *New York Daily News*, October 14, 2009.

20. Humbert S. Nelli, "Italians," in *Harvard Encyclopedia of American Ethnic Groups*, eds. Stephen Thernstrom, Ann Orlov, and Oscar Handlin (Cambridge, MA: Harvard University Press, 1980), 548.

21. "Special Report: America's Hispanics," *Economist*, March 14, 2015.

22. George J. Borjas, "The Slowdown in the Economic Assimilation of Immigrants: Aging and Cohort Effects Revisited Again," *Journal of Human Capital* 9 (2015).

23. "Those Assimilating Immigrants," *Wall Street Journal*, October 7, 2015.

24. Julia Preston, "Newest Immigrants Assimilating as Fast as Previous Ones, Report Says," *New York Times*, September 21, 2015.

25. Mary C. Waters and Marisa Gerstein Pineau, eds., *The Integration of Immigrants into American Society* (Washington, DC: National Academies Press, September 21, 2015), 6-12, 7-6 to 7-7.

Chapter 6.

1. Quoted in Philip Gleason, "American Identity and Americanization," in *Harvard Encyclopedia of American Ethnic Groups*, eds. Stephan Thernstrom, Ann Orlov, and Oscar Handlin (Cambridge, MA: Harvard University Press, 1980), 33.

2. Madison Grant, *The Passing of the Great Race: Or, The Racial Basis of European History* (New York: Scribner's Sons, 1916), 89.

3. Madison Grant, "Introduction to the Fourth Edition," in *The Passing of the Great Race* (New York: Scribner's Sons, 1922), xxviii.

4. "Modern Immigration Wave Brings 59 Million to U.S., Driving Population Growth and Change through 2065" (Pew Research Center, September 28, 2015).

5. "America's Assimilating Hispanics," *Wall Street Journal*, June 18, 2013.

6. Robert J. Samuelson, "Conspiracy against Assimilation," *Washington Post*, April 20, 2006.

7. Lydia Warren, "Meet the Four Immigrant Students Each Accepted to All Eight Ivy League Schools," DailyMail.com, April 20, 2015.

8. George J. Borjas, "The Intergenerational Mobility of Immigrants," *Journal of Labor Economics* 11 (1993).

9. Robert Park, *Race and Culture* (Glencoe, IL: Free Press, 1975); Richard Alba and Victor Nee, *Remaking the American Mainstream: Assimilation and Contemporary Immigration* (Cambridge, MA: Harvard University Press, 2005).

10. Quoted in Gleason, "American Identity and Americanization," 43.

11. Nathan Glazer and Daniel P. Moynihan, *Beyond the Melting Pot: The Negroes, Puerto Ricans, Jews, Italians, and Irish of New York City* (Cambridge, MA: MIT Press, 1963), xcvii.

12. Brian Duncan and Stephen J. Trejo, "Intermarriage and the Intergenerational Transmission of Ethnic Identity and Human Capital for Mexican Americans," *Journal of Labor Economics* 29 (2011); Brian Duncan and Stephen J. Trejo, "Assessing the Socioeconomic Mobility and Integration of U.S. Immigrants and Their Descendants," *Annals of the American Academy of Political and Social Science* 657 (2015).

13. George J. Borjas, "Ethnic Capital and Intergenerational Mobility," *Quarterly Journal of Economics* 107 (1992).

14. Olof Åslund et al., "Peers, Neighborhoods, and Immigrant Student Achievement: Evidence from a Placement Policy," *American Economic Journal: Applied Economics* 3 (2011).

15. Edward E. Telles and Vilma Ortiz, *Generations of Exclusion: Mexican Americans, Assimilation, and Race* (New York: Russell Sage Foundation, 2009).

16. Kathleen M. Conzen, "Germans," in *Harvard Encyclopedia of American Ethnic Groups*, 423; Humbert S. Nelli, "Italians," in *Harvard Encyclopedia of American Ethnic Groups*, 558.

17. "Tool: Recognizing Microaggressions and the Messages They Send" (University of California, Office of the President, 2015).

Chapter 7.

1. Daniel Griswold, "Introduction: Is Immigration Good for America?" *Cato Journal*, Winter 2012, 2; Sam Fulwood III, "Race and Beyond: Why Immigration Reform Is Good for All" (Center for American Progress, September 10, 2014); "Immigrants and Immigration: Answering the Tough Questions" (American Federation of State, County, and Municipal Employees, undated); "Foreign Workers Fill Hundreds of Sacramento-Area IT Jobs" (ABC10-TV, February 24, 2015).

2. Evan Pérez and Corey Dade, "Reversal of Fortune: An Immigration Raid Aids Blacks—for a Time," *Wall Street Journal*, January 17, 2007.

3. James Boswell and David Womersley, *The Life of Samuel Johnson* (New York: Penguin Classics, 2008), 612.

4. Pérez and Dade, "Reversal of Fortune."

5. David Card, "The Impact of the Mariel Boatlift on the Miami Labor Market," *Industrial and Labor Relations Review* 43 (1990).

6. Ibid., 252.

7. "The Economic Effects of Administrative Action on Immigration" (Council of Economic Advisers, November 2014), 9–10.

8. George J. Borjas, Richard B. Freeman, and Lawrence F. Katz, "How Much Do Immigration and Trade Affect Labor Market Outcomes," *Brookings Papers on Economic Activity* 1 (1997).

9. George J. Borjas, "The Labor Demand Curve *Is* Downward Sloping: Reexamining the Impact of Immigration on the Labor Market," *Quarterly Journal of Economics* 127 (2003).

10. Roger Lowenstein, "The Immigration Equation," *New York Times Magazine*, July 9, 2006.

11. George J. Borjas, "The Wage Impact of the *Marielitos*: A Reappraisal," National Bureau of Economic Research Working Paper No. 21588, September 2015.

12. Card, "Impact of the Mariel Boatlift," 249; emphasis added.

13. Niraj Chokshi, "Why Immigration May Not Have a Big Impact on Wages," *National Journal*, May 2, 2013.

14. George J. Borjas and Lawrence F. Katz, "The Evolution of the Mexican-Born Workforce in the United States," in *Mexican Immigration to the United States*, ed. George J. Borjas (Chicago: University of Chicago Press, 2007), 50; emphasis in original.

15. Frederick Douglass, *My Bondage and My Freedom* (New York: Dover, 1969), 454–55.

16. Bryan Caplan, "Are Low-Skilled Americans the Master Race?" *Library of Economics and Liberty*, March 28, 2006.

17. Gianmarco I. P. Ottaviano and Giovanni Peri, "Rethinking the Effects of Immigration on Wages," National Bureau of Economic Research Working Paper no. 12497, August 2006.

18. "Immigration's Economic Impact" (Council of Economic Advisers, June 20, 2007), 4.

19. George J. Borjas, Jeffrey Grogger, and Gordon H. Hanson, "Imperfect Substitution between Immigrants and Natives: A Reappraisal," National Bureau of Economic Research Working Paper no. 13887, March 2008.

20. Gianmarco I. P. Ottaviano and Giovanni Peri, "Rethinking the Effects of Immigration on Wages," *Journal of the European Economic Association* 10 (2012).

21. Ethan Lewis, "Immigration and Production Technology," *Annual Reviews of Economics* 5 (2013): 169.

22. David Card, "Immigration and Inequality," *American Economic Review* 99 (2009).

23. Patricia Cortés and Jessica Pan, "Foreign Nurse Importation to United States and the Supply of Native Registered Nurses," *Journal of Health Economics* 37 (2014), 164.

24. Bernt Bratsberg and Oddbjørn Raaum, "Immigration and Wages: Evidence from Construction," *Economic Journal* 122 (2012).

25. Giovanni Peri and Vasil Yasenov, "The Labor Market Effects of a Refu-

gee Wave: Applying the Synthetic Control Method to the Mariel Boatlift," National Bureau of Economic Research Working Paper no. 21801, December 2015.

26. George J. Borjas, "The Wage Impact of the *Marielitos*: Additional Evidence," National Bureau of Economic Research Working Paper no. 21850, January 2016.

27. Peri and Yasenov, "Labor Market Effects of a Refugee Wave," 37.

Chapter 8.

1. "The 'New American' Fortune 500" (Partnership for the American Economy, 2011); "Patent Pending: How Immigrants Are Reinventing the American Economy" (Partnership for the American Economy, 2012); Jean Leon Boucher, "The Nobel Prize: Excellence among Immigrants" (Institute for Immigration Research, George Mason University, November 2013).

2. Matthew Denhart, Growth and Immigration: A Handbook of Vital Immigration and Economic Growth Statistics (George W. Bush Institute, December 4, 2012), 8; "Immigration Reform: Implications for Growth, Budgets, and Housing" (Bipartisan Policy Center, October 2013); Juan Carlos Guzmán and Raúl C. Jara, "The Economic Benefits of Passing the DREAM Act" (Center for American Progress, October 2012).

3. George J. Borjas, "The Economic Benefits from Immigration," *Journal of Economic Perspectives* 9 (Spring 1995).

4. Fabian Waldinger, "Quality Matters: The Expulsion of Professors and the Consequences for Ph.D. Student Outcomes in Nazi Germany," *Journal of Political Economy* 118 (2010).

5. Fabian Waldinger, "Peer Effects in Science: Evidence from the Dismissal of Scientists in Nazi Germany," *Review of Economic Studies* 79 (2012).

6. Gina Kolata, "Soviet Scientists Flock to U.S., Acting as Tonic for Colleges," *New York Times*, May 8, 1990.

7. Ibid.

8. Donald E. McClure, "Employment Experiences of 1990–1991 U.S. Institution Doctoral Recipients in the Mathematical Sciences," *AMS Notices* 42 (1995): 754.

9. George J. Borjas and Kirk B. Doran, "The Collapse of the Soviet Union and the Productivity of American Mathematicians," *Quarterly Journal of Economics* 127 (2012).

10. Timothy B. Lee, "Gates to Congress: Microsoft Needs More H-1B Visas," *Ars Technica*, May 13, 2008.

11. William R. Kerr and William F. Lincoln, "The Supply Side of Innovation: H-1B Visa Reforms and U.S. Ethnic Invention," *Journal of Labor Economics* 28 (2010).

12. "Foreign Workers Fill Hundreds of Sacramento-Area IT Jobs" (ABC10-TV, February 24, 2015).

13. Giovanni Peri, Kevin Shih, and Chad Sparber, "STEM Workers, H-1B

Visas, and Productivity in US Cities," *Journal of Labor Economics* 33 (2015): S227.

14. Kirk B. Doran, Alexander M. Gelber, and Adam Isen, "The Effects of High-Skilled Immigration on Firms: Evidence from H-1B Visa Lotteries," National Bureau of Economic Research Working Paper no. 20668, November 2014.

15. Julia Preston, "Pink Slips at Disney. But First, Training Foreign Replacements," *New York Times*, June 3, 2015.

Chapter 9.

1. Quoted in Alex Nowrasteh, "Liberals Need to Choose: Welfare State or Immigration," *Huffington Post*, March 2, 2012.

2. "Friedman on Immigration and the Welfare State," *Open Borders: The Case* (blog), undated, http://openborders.info.

3. Quoted in Stephen Moore, "What Would Milton Friedman Say?" *Wall Street Journal*, May 29, 2013.

4. Maria Santana, "5 Immigration Myths Debunked" (CNN Money, November 20, 2014).

5. Jack Martin and Eric A. Ruark, "The Fiscal Burden of Illegal Immigration on United States Taxpayers" (Federation for American Immigration Reform, February 2011), 1.

6. "Those Assimilating Immigrants," *Wall Street Journal*, October 7, 2015.

7. John L. Czajka and Gabrielle Denmead, "Income Data for Policy Analysis: A Comparative Assessment of Eight Surveys" (US Department of Health and Human Services, December 2008).

8. George J. Borjas and Stephen J. Trejo, "Immigrant Participation in the Welfare System," *Industrial and Labor Relations Review* 44 (1991).

9. James P. Smith and Barry Edmonston, eds., *The New Americans: Economic, Demographic, and Fiscal Effects of Immigration* (Washington, DC: National Academy Press, 1997), 292–93.

10. Steven A. Camarota and Karen Zeigler, "The Declining Fertility of Immigrants and Natives" (Center for Immigration Studies, March 2015).

11. Smith and Edmonston, *New Americans*, 347.

12. "Immigration's Economic Impact" (Council of Economic Advisers, June 20, 2007).

13. Smith and Edmonston, *New Americans*, 325.

14. Betsy McCaughey, "ObamaCare Is Entering Its Dreaded 'Death Spiral,'" *New York Post*, October 19, 2015.

Chapter 10.

1. From the movie *Bananas* (1971).

Index

Page numbers in *italics* refer to tables.

DISCARD